tide and undertow

A Book of Translations

Anthony Weir

Blackstaff Press Belfast

Published by Blackstaff Press Limited, 16 Donegall Square South, Belfast, BT1 5JF, with the assistance of the Arts Council of Northern Ireland.

In Memory of
Shep
A Translator of Joy

SBN 85640 006 8

Printed in Northern Ireland by Belfast Litho Printers Limited.

E5

Translation is like the wrong side of an oriental carpet.
                                            Tolstoi

If you can't have thrushes to eat, then you must make do with blackbirds.
                                            French Proverb

A faithful translation is, like a faithful woman, never beautiful.
                                            Voltaire

Contents

Acknowledgements

I am most grateful to Carl Bagge for making available his Danish poems, and for introducing me to the poetry of Brecht; Lone Bruun Beyer for introducing me to the stories of Viggo Stuckenberg; Lars Huldén for making available his Swedish poems, and to Mikael Reuter for introducing me to them and helping with their translation; Jim Little for his patient help and advice with the Lisongo and Villon poems; Tom Matthews for his help with the Irish monastic poems, and to the literal prose translations of Dr Greene and 'Frank O'Connor' which introduced me to them; Grethe Risbjerg Thomsen for her suggestions regarding her own poems and for elucidating a Brecht poem for me; and to Mattie and Girlie who make the life of a poet and translator possible.

Anthony Weir

Thanks are due from the publishers to the following for permission to include some of the poems in this book:

To Gyldendal of Copenhagen for 'Recognition' p 57 and 'Eternal Triangle' p 52 by Tove Ditlevsen, 'The Word' p 53 and 'One Night Perhaps a March Night' p 54 by Grethe Risbjerg Thomsen, and 'Country Lass Unveiled' p 54 by Birthe Arnbak; to Lars Huldén for extracts from 'Enrönnen' pp 57-62 and 'Herr Varg!' p 62; to Stefan Brecht and Suhrkamp Verlag for 'Concerning a Drowned Girl' p 64 and 'Surabaya Johnny' p 65 © Suhrkamp Verlag Frankfurt am Main 1960, 'Ballad of the Jew-Lover Marie Sanders' p 67 © Suhrkamp Verlag Frankfurt am Main 1961, 'The Ballad of the Lady and the Forester' p 68 © Suhrkamp Verlag Frankfurt am Main 1964, 'Elephant Song' p 69 copyright 1955 by Suhrkamp Verlag Frankfurt am Main, 'Whore's Song' p 90 © Suhrkamp Verlag Frankfurt am Main 1957, all rights reserved; 'Ladies Looking for Lice' p 81 from *Breaking and Entering* by X J Kennedy, published by Oxford University Press, reprinted by permission of the publisher; Brendan Kennelly for the 'The Viking Terror' p 82, from the *Penguin Book of Irish Verse*; 'The Bitter Wind is High Tonight' p 83 by Robin Flower from *The Irish Tradition* by permission of the Oxford University Press, Oxford; Fierce and Wild is the Wind Tonight' p 83 by James Carney from *Studies in Irish Literature* by permission of the Dublin Institute for Advanced Studies.

The publishers have made every effort to trace the owners of copyright material appearing in this book. In the event of any questions arising as to the use of such material, the publishers, while expressing regret for any error unconsciously made, will be pleased to make the necessary correction in any future edition.

Drafts of some of the translations have appeared in *The Honest Ulsterman*. Carl Bagge's 'These Storks are Here to be Seen' is included in *My Kind of Rhymes* compiled by John Smith and published by Burke Books Ltd., 1972

Introduction

Some verse-translations defeat their own purpose by failing to capture the essence and flow of the originals; others fail because they so change or misinterpret the originals that their renderings can at best be called paraphrases, and at worst perversions. In one sense, a literal (prose) translation (preferably accompanying the original text) is, as Vladimir Nabokov maintained, 'a thousand times better than the prettiest paraphrase.' But it may sometimes be even more difficult to make a literal prose translation than a verse translation (see Appendix II) and, in any case, a truly inspired verse translation can match the original (as in Roy Campbell's renderings of the poems of St John of the Cross, or in Graeme Wilson's translations of the poems of Hagiwara), and a truly poetic re-creation, such as Fitzgerald's justly-celebrated 'translation' of Omar Khayyám, can even far surpass it.

I have tried to tread the dangerous path between literalness on the one hand and readability on the other. I have been anxious to keep as closely as possible to the literal meaning *and form* of the originals, simply because so many verse-translators have failed through too capricious paraphrase or interpretation of the original - for example, Yeats' famous paraphrase of Ronsard's even more famous sonnet.

At the same time I have been very conscious of the necessity to avoid my translations depending upon the reader knowing that they are translations - a suspension of disbelief - to make them acceptable.

One of the great problems in verse translation is to decide what can, if necessary, be left out, and what can, if absolutely necessary, be added to the original for the sake of rhyme, clarity, fluidity or intelligibility in English. 'Purists' should bear in mind that a poet almost certainly would have expressed himself or herself differently in another language, for different rhymes and rhythms would have presented themselves. It is not necessarily a disservice to the original poems, therefore, to make small omissions and changes to the literal meaning *provided that the whole resulting*

1

poem comes close to the spirit and meaning of the original.
Many verse-translations (especially those from Irish) have failed
because of a pedantic adherence to rhyme and metre into which
the translators try to wrench and cram the English.

I very much regret that space forbids inclusion of the original
poems, for I believe that a translation can fairly be judged only
alongside the original; and the inevitable shortcomings of trans-
lation can largely be offset by savouring the sounds of the original,
even if the language is unintelligible. But I make no apology for
the randomness of the selection of poems I have translated: even
a single poet's work is a random output, and *any* selection is
arbitrary by definition. I have not attempted to translate poems
according to a 'theme', but merely those that I both liked and
felt I had some measure of success in translating.

Certainly, I feel that the 'peripheral' literatures of Ireland,
Scandinavia, etc., and oral or 'folk' poetry everywhere, should be
better known and held in much higher regard. I hope that this
book will help to overcome a snobbery that also ignores mediaeval
Irish, Scandinavian and Mongol art, and treats all non-European
and non-'Mainstream' art with condescension. At the same time,
however, the very greatest poets - such as Rimbaud and Villon -
must constantly be celebrated and kept as a standard by which
other poetry can be measured.

I have been concerned only to make translations which do
justice in some measure to originals scattered in time between
the third millennium BC and the present century, and in place
between the rain forests of the Zaïre basin and the wild coasts of
Ireland - tears that are tides of joy or undertows of desolation.

Anthony Weir

Kilnatierney
Autumn 1973

From the Irish

Early Irish Monastic Poetry (Eighth to Twelfth Centuries)

Although Ireland was substantially Christian by the beginning of the sixth century (Christianity having reached its shores a century or more earlier), pagan Celtic and pre-Celtic rituals, cults and beliefs survived a long time - and indeed still survive, often under a Christian guise. Goddesses, warriors and heroes of pre-Christian times did not disappear with the coming of a would-be pacifist and monotheistic religion, but gradually turned into miraculous saints and hermits, usually by the transference of their qualities to monks and nuns bearing the same names. Christianity had to compromise to survive in an island inhabited by tribes of the most warlike peoples known to history: the Celts who occupied much of western and central Europe, and whose cults and mysteries were as dark and violent as the message of Christianity purported to be sweet and light. And, indeed, perhaps two thousand years earlier, the Celts also Irishised themselves in their new and very traditional homeland, just as the Normans did seven hundred years later. Thus the Irish triple-goddess Brighíd became *Saint* Brigid, and pagan cult sites (like religious offices) were taken over by the new cult, or

"Sheila-na-gig", Kiltihane Church, County Tipperary.

were associated with some miraculous overthrow, usually by St Patrick or (ironically) St Brigid, of the earlier religions (personified vaguely by the term 'demons'). So Altadaven in county Tyrone, where there is a 'St Patrick's' (also known as 'St Brigid's') Well, means 'The Demons' Cliff' - over which St Patrick (or St Brigid) cast the devils of the powers of pagan 'darkness'; and this legend is the measure of the importance of the site in pre-Christian times. Even today the old cult-rock of 'Spink-ana-gaev' ('Pinnacle Rock') dark under the trees, seems like a portal to the Otherworld, and Lughnasa (Lammas) celebrations were held here until recently.

In county Cork there is still a tradition of 'Saint' Gobnait, who still, after 1,500 years of Christianity, has not been quite entirely absorbed by the Church. Her 'Pattern' continues, despite clerical disapproval, and her miraculous powers of healing are still sought: the crutches of the cured may be seen on 'St Gobnait's Grave' at Ballyvourney. That she was of some importance at least in Iron Age if not in Bronze Age Celtic times is suggested by the survival of her name in at least three widely-separated places: Kilgobnet (Gobnait's Church) in county Kerry, Kilgobnet in county Waterford, and Kilgobnet on Inisheer, Aran. She is associated with Nature's most beautiful fertiliser, the bee.

Gobnait the Abbess replaced her namesake, who was, like the *Caillech Bhéarra,* a local manifestation of the Celtic 'Divine Hag'. 'Cailleach Bhéarra's House' is the name for pre-historic gallery-graves in county Sligo, county Louth and county Waterford; and 'Cailleach Bhéarra's Lough' stands dark and forbidding on top of one of Ireland's most mythologi-cal mountains: Slieve Gullion in county Armagh, where there is a passage-grave from which can be seen (on a good day!) Slieve na Calliagh (Hag's Mountain), thirty miles to the south-west, where there is a spectacular passage-grave cemetery.

The *Cailleach Bhéarra* is, moreover, the subject of one of the finest poems in Irish. From a powerful and sexually-potent Celtic and perhaps pre-Celtic goddess, wife of the great god Lúgh, who herself controlled land, seasons and fertility, she survives through time transformed in the poem to a sort of latter-day Mary Magdalen asking Christ to share her bed. The little provocatively-female stone figures known as 'Sheila-na-gigs' (*Cíog* means 'pap' in Irish) and which are sometimes found built into early stone churches as at Kiltinane in county Tipperary, or into mediaeval castles as at Bunratty in county Clare and Dunnaman in county Limerick, may be connected with the Cailleach Bhéarra or her local counterparts. One used to be known locally as 'The Witch', and others as 'Evil Eye Stones', some may be considerably more recent than the 11th century poem on the 'Nun' of Beare included in this anthology.

In county Cork one of the most impressive of prehistoric wedge-shaped gallery-graves (100 feet long) is called Labbacallee (Leaba Caillighe: The Hag's Bed)...

So it is not surprising that the earliest Irish monastic poems are still strongly influenced by pre-Christian beliefs, particularly as earlier religion placed great emphasis on Trinity, a concept which may have acted as a kind of bridge between the two world-views. The great Irish High Crosses as late as the twelfth century incorporated motifs which owe as much to the ancient Scythians and the eastern Mediterranean as to Scandinavian or 'indigenous' influences. Indeed the term 'Irish' has little meaning beyond the geographical. Motifs occuring in Irish sculpture occur also as far east as China, and Irish poems often had Continental models. At the same time Ireland is a remarkable repository of ancient and even prehistoric patterns of thought and behaviour: the essence of Ireland is ancient *and* eclectic.

The well-known Litany or 'Breastplate of St Patrick', which has been paraphrased into a hymn with a stirring tune, is a basically Christian 'Breastplate' with pagan elements tacked on to it for respectability's sake in the form of a protective charm in the early rhythmic style - just as old statues were incorporated into the early stone Christian churches. Another 'Breastplate' also from the eighth century, is, on the other hand, a pagan spell with a piece of Christianity tacked on - not for respectability's, but more likely, novelty's sake - to the end.

'Breastplate'

I call upon the Seven Daughters of the Sea
who spin the fine threads of longevity;
may three deaths be taken from me,
may three lives be given to me,
seven waves of wealth poured for me.
May ghosts not harm me as I journey
in my bright, untarnished Breastplate.
May my name be not pledged in vain,
may death not come to me till I am old.

I call upon my Silver Champion
who has not died and will not die;
may time like bronze be granted to me
as bright as bronze and of like quality.

May my state be exalted,
may my law be ennobled,
may my strength be augmented,
may my tomb not be readied,
nor my journey be final,
my return be assured me.
May I not be assailed by the two-headed snake
nor the hard grey worm
nor the senseless slug.
May no thief attack me
nor a host of women
nor a host of warriors.
May I have increase of time
from the King of all things.

I call on Senach of the Seven Lives
suckled by witches on the breasts of Luck;
may my seven candles not be quenched.

I am an invincible fortress.
I am an immoveable rock.
I am a precious stone.
I am the symbol of the Seven Riches.

5

May I have hundreds of possessions,
hundred of years,
hundred after hundred.

I summon my Luck to me;
may the Grace of the Holy Spirit be upon me.
Domini est salus
Christi est salus
Super populum tuum, Domine benedictio tua.

[The Irish texts I have used for the Translations are mostly as published in *A Golden Treasury of Irish Poetry, AD 600 to 1200* by Greene and O'Connor, published by Macmillan, London, 1967. A select Bibliography of Irish poetry and history appears in Appendix I, after comparisons of different translations of Irish poetry.

An excellent introduction to Irish and other Celtic literature is provided by Kenneth Hurlstone Jackson's *A Celtic Miscellany*, published by Penguin Books.]

From 'The Voyage of Bran'

This eighth-century extract is a remarkable intermingling of Christian and pagan-Celtic imagery in a double vision of the sea and the Earthly Paradise, showing something of the Celtic concept of the relativity of place, time and substance.

Manannán Mac Lír in the fourth verse is the sea-god (or husband of the sea) associated with the Isle of Man and the Isle of Arran and whose name and patronymic (but not his legend) is related to the Welsh god Manawydan fab Llŷr.

Bran is the name of an Ulster king-hero who made a voyage to Paradise and the Land of the Women, during which he met the sea-god driving his chariot across the waves. The sea-god speaks 30 stanzas of verse, of which the first 12 and the last of the 28 which survive are translated below. They describe Paradise, variously called *Findargad* (White-silver), *Argadnel* (Silver Cloud), *Airgthech* (White Mansion), *Ciúin* (Peaceful), *Imchiúin* (Very Peaceful), *Magh Mon* (Plain of Sport), *Mag Meall* (Sweet Plain), and *Emnae, Emhain* or *Emhain Abhlach* (Emhain of the Apple Trees) which reappears in Arthurian legend in the form *Avalon,* and which is identified with the Isle of Arran in the Firth of Clyde. Bran is not to be confused (though he is not entirely unconnected) with St Brendan of Clonfert, 'The Navigator', famous in medieval times for sailing out in his little skin boat on the Atlantic in quest of the Otherworld. Bran (meaning 'raven') was the name also of one of Cú Chulainn's (the Irish equivalent of Gilgamesh or Hercules) dogs, and it is still widely used as a dog's name in Ireland.

But there is a different, Welsh, *Brân* or *Bendigeidfran*: 'Bran the Blessed', brother of Manawydan son of Llŷr, and a god - whereas the Irish Bran survived in the literature only as a hero. Manawydan, like the Irish Bran and Brendan, is connected with a raid on the Underworld. *Bran* is the P-Celtic (even though Irish is a Q-Celtic tongue) form of *Cronus* (crow) more familiar as the Roman god Saturn, and associated with the Alder-tree which, like the crow or raven, is a symbol of death. (After the sacrifice of a sacral king, a crow or raven was thought to house his soul, and on the tenth-century High Crosses at Durrow and Clonmacnoise in county Offaly, a raven is depicted with its beak in the mouth of the entombed Christ.) Brân and south-western England are both associated with the chough-dance in the maze - a western form of the partridge-dance in the Cretan Labyrinth.

Bran was wounded in the foot by a poisoned spear, and in a later Welsh tradition Bron was the Grail-bearer whom the Fisher-king castrated like Cronus, and who was cured only by a virgin warrior bearing a (phallic) bloodstained lance, whose healing power would turn a Waste Land of winter to the fertile soil of spring. The Bleeding Lance seems to have a prototype in Irish myth, being associated with Cú Chulainn.

According to Welsh tradition, Brân laid 50 maidens in a single night, perhaps a college of priestesses serving the Moon-goddess to whom the sacred king had access once a year during their orgies round a stone phallus such as the celebrated one from Turoe in county Galway. And after a Pyrrhic victory over the Irish, the Welsh Brân orders seven surviving warriors to cut off his head for burial at an oracular shrine on Tower Hill in London to protect the kingdom against invasion, just as, according to Ambrose (Epistle VII), Adam's head was buried at Golgotha to protect Jerusalem from the North. During the journey from Wales to London Brân's head provides the seven with as pleasant company as his whole body had done when alive, for it remains uncorrupted. (The cult of the severed head was important to the Celtic peoples - see my translation of 'The Song of the Heads'.)

Brân and Bran (Bron) are sun-heroes, although they are different branches of a common ancestral myth. And sun-heroes all, like Christ, Orpheus, Hercules, Osiris and the Irish Fionn Mac Cumhaill, harrow hell (in Danish Bronze Age engravings, boats and suns occur together).

Both Welsh and Irish branches of the Brân/Bran tradition finally unite in a new legend of King Arthur (who has striking resemblances to the Irish Fionn), sitting in the middle of a web of Neolithic and later fertility rites like an atavistic spider, or a central panel in the equally complex and eclectic pattern of fertility zoomorphs in an Irish manuscript - or indeed like the ravens perched upon the headless corpse that is borne on horseback in a strange procession led by a monk carrying a ringed cross, which is sculpted on the base of one of the marvellous eighth-century High Crosses at Ahenny in county Tipperary.

> A marvel of delight to Bran
> it seems to sail the clear green sea.
> In my curragh it's a plain
> of flowers that I travel free.
>
> It's water to the bright beaked boat
> that Bran's aboard. And to me
> in my two-wheeled chariot
> it is more Paradise than sea.
>
> Bran sees waves that fall and rise
> upon the ocean's clear green flesh.
> I see flowers in Paradise
> blooming bright without blemish.

Summer's sea-horses play
as far as Bran's blue eye can peer.
Streams of honey flow, away
in the Land of Manannán Mac Lír.

The glittering of the sea he sails,
the dazzling of the deep he rows
has poured forth blue and golden scales
from solid land on which he goes.

Salmon leap from white sea's womb
and they are calves, and they are lambs
in peace without a butchered doom,
the dancing calves, the frisking lambs.

Though you see in Paradise
but one horseman among the flowers,
there, hidden from your eyes
are many horses in its bowers.

The greatness of the Land of the West
and its host, is a stream
of silver and a golden beam
to bring joy at every feast.

A noble gathering, they play
pleasant games, and lose, or win.
Men and gentle women play
without fault or original sin.

Bran's boat sails upon a wood,
his little boat upon the seas.
Beneath its harvest a sweet wood,
beneath his prow the tops of trees.

A wood with flowers and with fruit
and the true smell of the vine;
no decay of limb nor rot of root
where golden leaves shimmer and shine.

From creation's dawn we have no age,
have no corruption of the earth.
No loss of strength comes with decay,
for Original Sin has not stained our birth.

Steadily then let Bran pull;
the Land of Women sweetly calls;
he'll reach the rich and bountiful
Isle of Joy before night falls.

The 'Nun' of Beare

Buí, a wife of the sky-god Lúgh, is another name for the *Caillech Bhéarra,* one of the
Celtic 'Divine Hags' of battle, territory, fertility and death, who were at the same time
ravishing and insatiable maiden-goddesses. In early Irish the word *caillech* meant an old
woman or hag, but it is used in this poem with overtones derived from the word *caille*
meaning a veil (particularly that of a nun), and in modern Irish *cailleach* can mean both
an old woman, and, secondarily, a nun. So memories of the enchantress and goddess that
she was mingle bitterly with the desolation of a woman cursing the barren old age of mor-
tality that has come with Christianity. In a last and hopeless bid to recover her lost power,
she wishes that Christ himself or, failing him, any man - would come to her in the ebb-
tide of her decline. She is indeed a lasting symbol of Ireland herself. 'Beare' is the name
of a rocky and wild peninsula (and an island off it) in west Cork.

She appears in genealogical tradition as the foster-mother of Corc Duibne, ancestor of
the Corcu Duibne ('People of Duibne') of the Kerry Peninsulas. (The Dingle Peninsula is
still called Corca Dhuibhne, or Corcaguiney.) Ogham memorial stones abounding in the
area bear this out by claiming a common ancestress, Dovinia.

This is perhaps the finest and most famous poem in Irish, and it seems to be an
eleventh-century hotch-potch of perhaps half-a-dozen poems on the same theme - and
hence it has presented considerable trouble for editors. It is a 'pseudo-saga': a poem in
the pre-Christian heroic tradition which concerned Christian people and events, treating
them with at least as great an extravagance sometimes as the heroes of pre-Christian myth
and legend - such as Fionn Mac Cumhaill ('Finn Mac Cool') who was associated with the
fertile plain of Femen around Cashel in county Tipperary, and its cult-mountain, Slieve-
namon. Mountain-tops are favourite sites for prehistoric *tumuli* containing passage graves
less elaborate than the celebrated lowland ones by the sacred river Boyne at Newgrange,
Knowth and Dowth in county Meath. Knowth, like the cairn-topped Slieve Gullion in
county Armagh, is closely associated with the *Cailleach Bhéarra,* whose antiquity may
stretch even beyond the Bronze Age which came with the first Celtic-speaking people
in Ireland, to the Stone Age peoples whose cults and cult-sites may have been taken
over and venerated by pagan Celts and by Christians after them. Knowth, like the
Cailleach Bhéarra, changed its function many times - from passage-grave complex to
inauguration site to tunnelled storehouse to Norman motte.

While trying to keep to the verse-order of the most important manuscript of the
poem, I have had to transpose a few verses here and there; and I have omitted a few

which are spoken by a man (apparently St Cuimíne Fota of Kerry, AD 592-662), and some which do not seem to have any connection at all with the 'Nun' of Beare.

I have used a three-line verse in English to render the starkness of the Irish quatrains, and I have tried to make a unified poem without attempting to reassemble the verses into any 'logical' order as some other translators have done. Indeed, the order in which they occur in the manuscript seems to me ideal. The last nine verses, however, clearly form a complete poem or section in themselves, though in the manuscript the first of these was transposed to the beginning of the whole collection of poems and fragments so as to match the desolate ending. I have retained it at the beginning as in the manuscript, and repeated it where it probably belonged originally.

Kuno Meyer, in his *Ancient Irish Poetry* translates the preface to the poem as follows:

"The Old Woman of Beare had seven periods of youth one after the other, so that every man who lived with her came to die of old age, and her grandsons and great-grandsons were tribes and races. For a hundred years she wore the veil which Cummin had blessed upon her head. Thereupon old age and infirmity came to her. 'Tis then she said:"

My life is ebbing; let it drain
unlike the sea which flows again.
Is mé Caillech Bhérri Buí.[†]

I whose gown was always new
am now so pitifully thin
that this old shift will outlive me.

They want only money now.
When we were young, love was what
we wanted - and so richly got.

People then were generous,
and in return they asked a lot.
They asked and give so little now.

I had chariots and horses then,
given by admiring kings.
I drank mead and wine with them...

Now among old onion-skins
of withered women I drink whey,
myself a withered onion-skin.

My hands are bony now, and thin;
once they plied their loving trade
upon the bodies of great kings.

My hands are bony, wasted things,
unfit to stroke an old man's head
much less a young man's glowing skin.

Young girls are happy in the Spring,
but I am sad and worse than sad,
for I'm an old and useless thing.

Nobody round me is glad;
my hair is grey and going thin.
This white veil hides what's well-hid.

I once had bright cloth on my head
and went with kings; now I dread
the going to the King of kings.

I hate all old things, except
for ancient Femen;* its old crown
is golden still - while I corrupt.

An age of storms has beaten down
on Femen, but its cheeks have kept
their bloom, unlike my own.

The Winter winds ravish the sea.
No nobleman will visit me,
no - not even a slave will come.

It's long ago I sailed the sea
of youth and beauty wantonly.
Now my passion too has gone.

Even in Summer I wear a shawl -
it's many a day since I was warm.
The Summer of youth has turned to Fall.

Wintry age's smothering pall
is wrapping slowly round my limbs.
My hair's like lichen, my breasts like galls.

I'm glad of my youth's lust and rage,
for even had I been demure
I still would wear the cloak of age.

The cloak that distant hillsides wear
is beautiful; their foliage
is woven with eternal care.

I am old; the eyes that once
burned bright for men are now decayed:
the torch has burned out its sconce.

*See page 9 above.

My life is ebbing; let it drain
unlike the sea which flows again.
Is mé Caillech Bhérri Buí. †

Flow and ebb: what the flow brings
the ebb soon takes away again -
the flow and the ebb following.

The flow and the ebb following:
the flow's joy and the ebb's pain;
the flow's honey, the ebb's sting.

The flow has not quite flooded me;
there is a recess still quite dry
though many were my company.

Well might God's son come to me
in my recess - could I deny
a man my only hospitality?

A hand is laid upon them all
whose ebb always succeeds their flow
whose rising sinks into their fall.

If my veiled and sunken eyes
could see more than their own ebb
there's nothing they would recognise.

Happy the island of the sea
where flow always comes after ebb.
No flow will follow ebb in me.

I am wretched. What was flow
is now all ebb. Ebbing I go.
After the tide, the undertow.

†I am Buí, the 'Nun' of Beare.

King Sweeney

King Suibhne, or Sweeney, was a fictional East Ulster king who, supposedly cursed by 'Saint' Ronan, 'went mad' during the battle of Moira (Mag Roth) in 637 AD and took refuge in the forest.

The first of these two poems, a ninth-century fragment from the same manuscript as 'Cat and Monk', is a fine statement of sanity.

One of the peculiarities or insular Celtic Christianity was the intimacy between God and monk. Very often, as in this poem, God is called 'darling'. (See also the intimate language used by Mael Isu when addressing his long-lost prayer-book.)

King Sweeney's 'Oratory'

No great household could ever be
finer than my Oratory here
where sun and moon and stars of Tuaim Inbhir[1]
shine soft and bright above my tree.

It was a great Craftsman[2] made
my Oratory - it was even
darling God in Heaven
who thatched my roof, my shade.

A house where no rain comes,
a place that's safe from spears,
as bright as in a garden - and no fears
where no fence runs.

The second of these two poems, dating from the twelfth century, comes from the pseudo-saga 'Buile Suibhne' - 'The Madness of Sweeney', a narrative containing several poems about him, some like the poems below, expressing joy in his forest solitude, others bewailing his wretchedness. See also Appendix III for a monkish account of the rigours of solitude.

Thus: Little antlered one, little belling one,
melodious little bleater,
nothing could be sweeter
than your lowing in the glen...

and: Though sweet in your church yonder
to hear your students murmur,
it is sweeter in Glen Bolcain
with the wolves' splendid talking...

compared with:

Falling down from rotten boughs,
roaming through the prickly whins,
shunning men, befriending wolves,
running with stags across the plain;

sleeping without a quilt at night
in the crest of a bushy tree,
never hearing human voice -
O Christ, it is all grief to me!...

and:

The wind is icy,
the sun blear.
A lone tree shelter
on the flat moor...

The text of these extracts is not in Green and O'Connor (op cit) but in J G O'Keeffe's *Buile Shuibne*, London 1913.

Excellent prose translations of parts of the Buile Shuibhne are included in Kenneth Hurlstone Jackson's *A Celtic Miscellany* (Penguin Books, 1971) - numbers 23, 24, 205, 206 and 207.

In the extract which follows, I found that (as in *The 'Nun' of Beare*) the succinctness and starkness of the original was better preserved in English by using a three-line verse (except in the last verse) rather than the quatrains of the original.

King Sweeney's Solitude

The trees are now my shelter;
the Bann cuckoo calls sweeter
than any church-bell's sound.

As flax is scutched by women
so was my army beaten
on the plain of Mag Roth.

From the cliffs of Loch Diolair[3]
to Derry Colum Chille
there are no swans at war.

The lonely stag is belling;
there is no music dwelling
more sweetly in my heart.

15

Christ! Christ, hear me!
O Christ without trace
of sin - Christ, love me!
deny me not your grace.

1. *Tuaim Inbhir* (or Toominveer) might most accurately be translated as 'Mon Repos', since it means 'a hiding place', 'a place of refuge'. There was, apparently, a monastery of this name in the western part of the ancient kingdom of Meath, roughly about the middle of Ireland.

2. The Irish text has *Gobbán*, a late form of *Goibhniú*, the Celtic smith god.

3. It is not possible to identify this lough (which rhymes with 'miller'). Mention of cliffs may make it a sea-lough or inlet - perhaps in Sligo or south Donegal - whose name has since changed. On the other hand, it may be connected with *Droim Diolair* ('Drum' is a common component in Irish place-names denoting a ridge or small hill) which the editor of *Buile Shuibhne* located near Belleek on the Fermanagh-Donegal border - where, however, there are no cliffs. (Information by courtesy of the Irish Placenames Commission.)

Líadan and Cuirithir

Líadan and Cuirithir were two famous Irish lovers, beloved of pseudo-saga writers. The Connacht poet Cuirithir came to marry the Cork poetess Líadan, who was a daughter of an important ecclesiastical family - only to find that she had become a nun in compliance with her parents' wishes. He in turn became a monk, but as their ecclesiastically-unacceptable love did not diminish, they put themselves under the tutelage of Cummíne of Clonfert to cure themselves of their love. He took the drastic step of submitting them to a 'test of intimacy' by making them sleep together with an acolyte between them - without success!(Poor acolyte.)Finally, Cuirithir left in frustration (religious or sexual or both) to go on a pilgrimage, leaving Líadan to lament.

One of the words in Irish for 'monk' was 'ex-warrior' or 'ex-layman', which makes the first of these three poems ironic. They date from the eighth century.

The Ex-Poet

South of the church there stands a stone
where the ex-poet sat alone;
I go at twilight, after prayer,
sad to be without him for ever.

The former poet, Cuirithir,
loved me, and I loved him dear
though I got no good of it.
Dear is the lord of the two grey feet!*

He will have no heifer bulled,
no cow; no thighbone will be lulled
by the right hand of Cuirithir
the former poet I loved dear.

*This curious line refers to Cuirithir's father whose name meant 'Otter' in Irish - though the four feet of the otter are definitely more brown than grey (the word in Irish can also mean 'bright', 'blue' and 'green'!) It may be, of course, that some at any rate of Irish otters in the eighth century were darker - more a charcoal than a dark chestnut colour; and some reports of Irish otters in the past mention a darker colour (see C J Harris: *Otters, a study of the recent Lutrinae*, London 1968). On the other hand, an albino otter might have been in the poet's mind.

Líadan

I have angered one
I love. Joyless to me
is the thing I've done.

I'd be mad
not to do what pleased him
- but for fear of God.

What I'll win:
to by-pass Hell to Paradise
is no loss to him.

The man
I loved is Cuirithir
My name is Líadan.

A silliness
angered Cuirithir with me;
I treated him with gentleness.

A short time
only we were together -
and it was sublime.

The forest rang
when I was with Cuirithir
and the blue sea sang.

No vow
I made should have angered
him against me now.

I'll not conceal
he was my heart's true love
though I loved the Universe as well.

My heart
is riven by a flame. It will
not hold now we are apart.

The Trial of Intimacy

Cuirithir:
I am to spend a night this way:
chaste with Líadan, you say.
No fool would waste the night with her
if he were man, and secular.

Líadan:
I am to spend a night this way
with Cuirithir. Though we lay
together and apart a year
we still should hold the ordeal dear!

The Monk Mael Ísu Rediscovers his Psalm Book

Beginning in language of less than courtly love and ending in a passion of religious zeal, this poem disarmingly reveals centuries before Freud and his followers the sexual nature of religiosity, which, in Mael Ísu's case, is quite unrepressed.

My old flame! though you're young no more
you're still as virginal and true
as when we met on Lough Neagh's shore
and I slept easily with you.

When we had our first night of joy
you were wise and a sharp young maid,
and I was just a simple boy
of seven, simple as a spade.

In Ireland's great world far and wide
pure in flesh and mind we've tramped,
and still my love is undefiled,
a wild, pure fire that burns undamped.

You've been with four men since we slept
together last - and ever true
and free from sin and shame you've kept,
I see and know as all men do.

And now again at last we've found
each other; and on every page
your ready counsel's still as sound
as ever, though you're dark with age.

I love you blamelessly - and this
is my glad welcome, O my love.
You'll keep me from the black Abyss
and lead me to the Light above.

The world between for far and wide
is full of your resounding fame,
and I will surely reach God's side
if I burn brightly with your flame.

To every man on earth you give
your testimony; and you say
that it is no lie to live
to pray Our Father every day.

May God grant it me to spend
my years with you in peace of mind,
and may He let my soul ascend
when my bent body's left behind.

Cat and Monk

This famous and much-translated ninth-century poem is scribbled on the margin of a manuscript preserved in the Monastery of St Paul in Carinthia. A facsimile of the script is reproduced in Ludwig Bieler's *Ireland: Harbinger of the Middle Ages* published by the Oxford University Press (p 44).

My cat, white Pangur, and myself
are each at work: he with stealth
is hunting mice, while I
pursue philosophy.

I envy no man - I prefer
my scholarship to worldly care;
and he would rather stalk his prey
than hunt what I hunt every day.

At home, alone, our lives are tales
without monotony; the different skills
that we employ
compose our world - a world of joy.

After desperate struggle lies
a mouse between his paws - and dies.
I struggle to make head or tail
of something challenging in my travail.

On the corner Pangur's eye
is fixed with fierce intensity;
and my own, though not so keen,
is set on knowledge still unseen.

He runs round with pride and joy
when his claws close on his prey.
I am happy too when I
have solved a problem dear to me.

However long we are together
neither will disturb the other.
Alone with happy concentration
each purses his occupation.

pursues

The job that he does every day
he's fitted for; in the same way
I am competent and right
in turning darkness into light.

Winter

Hear my news:
the stag bells loud;
Winter snows
are Summer's shroud.

The cold wind's high
and low the sun,
brief in the sky.
Big tides run.

The bracken's brown;
barnacle-geese
over the sound
cry to the ice.

Cold has caught
the wings of birds.
Ice has brought
my winter words.

Ironically, the warlike Irish Celts, once Christianised, soon had to withstand the depredations of the Norsemen, whose paganism was similar to the Celtic mysteries. The great inland monastery of Clonmacnois on the Shannon was sacked and burned no less than nine times throughout its history by the warring Irish (as well as by not always united invaders), and was finally destroyed by the English in the sixteenth century.

Storm in Uncertain Times†

The winds are bitter tonight; they tear
and wildly toss the sea's white hair.
And yet they bring my mind much ease
for Norsemen sail on calmer seas.

†See Appendix I.

The Sea in Swell*

Look to the West	*Fégaid úaib*
where whales caress	*sair fo-thúaid*
the sea's unrest	*in muir muaid*
unceasing;	* mílach;*
gymnasium	*adba rón*
of seals that swim	*rebach ran*
the sea's abrim	*ro gab lán*
and seething.	* línad.*

*Like one of the fragments about the Blackbird at Belfast Lough, this eleventh or twelfth century poem is an alliterative, stressed metre borrowed from a Latin model. Some French poems of about this time are in an identical form.

Exiles

Happy those who take their lovers
in a boat with sturdy rowers
long-prowed, high and proud as towers
from the country of their mothers.

The Song of the Heads

Cormac mac Cuileannáin, scholar-king of Munster and Bishop of Cashel, was killed in 908 AD in the battle of Belagh Mughna (Balagh Moon) by Flann Sinna, king of Tara. Because Cormac was a scholar as well as a king-bishop, his death was the subject of much poetry, including this ballad from a twelfth-century romance. At the time of Cormac's death the strife between rival Irish petty-kingdoms accounted for nearly as much destruction (including churches and monasteries) as the raids of the Norsemen - who were also fighting among themselves and forming alliances with Irish kings. In the Irish, this poem obsessively repeats the word *'truagh'* in seven out of the nine verses. It means both 'pitiful', 'piteous', 'wretched', and 'weak'. I have used 'piteous' throughout, although clearly in some instances 'weak' would be more natural in English.

It should be remembered that decapitation was often a feature of 'Celtic' religion, and heads were as greatly prized as cult objects in Western Europe and the British Isles then, as recently by 'savages' in other parts of the world, and as the steam engine was in 19th century Europe or, to a lesser degree, the motor car is today.

It is piteous, King of Kings,
righteous King, O King of hosts.
Sadder than the saddest song
is the song of the heads in the dead of night.

Head of Geagán, come here,
join us in our piteous moan,
for we have pledged ourselves to sing
for the son of Cuileannáin.*

Three brothers were we yesterday,
in the host three strong proud men.
Tonight our three and severed heads
come lamenting piteously.

Ach, alas!
Though time is short, it's shorter still
for the King of clouds to make
strong men piteously weak.

The prince who strode into the field
encouraging his many hosts
gave us a bright apple each
and pledged us to our piteous song.

*i.e. Cormac

Ach, alas!
Cormac fell in the battlefield.
Now, since he has no seed,
Cashel's glory too is dead.

Cormac from the Mound of Kings
was noble Munster's noble King.
Everything he had to say
touched proud and piteous in the same way.

He was a great filler of vats,
he was a great cleaver of oaks,
and great at felling champions
and making proud the piteous.

Dawn has come - now cease your song:
it is time for silence now.
Say farewell tonight, and go
to join your piteous trunks again.

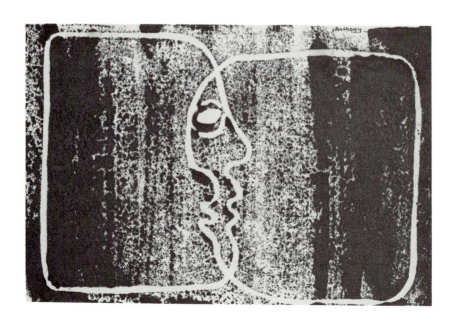

The Blackbird

This is a fusion of two unrelated fragments: *The Blackbird* (which appears in a margin of the Leabhar Breac or 'The Speckled Book') and *The Blackbird at Belfast Lough* (Loch Laíg). I have made the metre throughout that of the latter fragment, which appears in its entirety beside my re-creation. (See Appendix I).

A little bird
whistling loud
from beak-tip
   brightly yellow,
from a bough
of yellow flowers
has tossed a cry
   so mellow.

Blackbird
at Belfast Lough
you're happy in
   your singing,
hermit
who whistles sweet
no bell needs
   your ringing.

Int én bec
to léic feit
do rind guip
   glanbuidi,
fo-ceird faíd
ós Loch Laíg
lon do chraíb
   charrbuidi.

A Kiss

This brilliantly concise and simple poem literally means: 'He is my heart, my grove of nuts. He is my boy, and here's a kiss for him.' In Irish, the 'apple of one's eye' is the 'nut of one's heart', and 'heart' itself is the most usual word for 'love'. This raises problems in translation which I have not managed quite to solve.

He is my eye
   my apple-grove.
He is my boy
   and this
   a kiss
for my love.

Cride é
   daire cnó.
Ócán é
   pócán dó.

The Scribe

My hand is tired from writing,
unsteady is my pen.
Its slender beak is spouting
dark ink from the glen.

My little wet nib runs over
books that are thronged like a fair.
From the holly by the river
its ink is drawn with care.

An endless stream of wisdom
flows from me, as I stand,
for the wealth of princedom.
How tired is my hand!

From the French

Rondeau
(Anonymous, XIIIth century)

Is there a Paradise, my love,
any Paradise but loving?
Indeed there's not, my sweet darling.
Is there a Paradise, my love?
He who in his love's arms lies
indeed has found his Paradise.
Is there a Paradise, my love,
any Paradise but loving?

FRANÇOIS VILLON (1431-1463 or later)

Ballade of Ladies of Bygone Times[1]
from *The Testament* (1462)

Tell me from where I could entice
Flora the famous Roman whore,
or Archipiada, or Thaïs[2]
who they say was just as fair;
or Echo answering everywhere
across stream and pool and mere,
whose beauty was like none before
- where are the snows of yesteryear?

Where is the learned Héloïse
for whose love Abelard became
a gelded monk at Saint-Denis,
yet still could not put out the flame?
And where now is that royal dame[3]
who had men for three days with her
then had them cast into the Seine?
Where are the snows of yesteryear?

1. A Ballade was a poem which varied in form but usually consisted of three to five verses of eight to ten lines and a verse of four or five lines, with various rhyme-schemes.

2. Archipiada (*Archipiade* in French) is a mistake on Villon's part for Alcibiades, whom Boetius mentions as a paragon of beauty, and hence was assumed to be a woman in the days of courtly love.

3. The Queen who reputedly took lovers for three days, and then had them hurled into the Seine, was Jeanne of Navarre by one tradition, or Margaret of Burgundy (wife of Louis X) by another. The apocryphal story of the philosopher Buridan (c 1295 - c 1385) and how he arranged for a barge of hay to be stationed by fellow-students under the window or balcony from which he was to be flung, was much appreciated and elaborated from the XIVth to the XIXth century.

4. Blanche of Castile was the mother of Louis IX.

5. The Prince may be Villon's royal friend, Charles of Orléans (1394-1465) who was captured at Agincourt in 1415 and kept as a prisoner in England until 1440. He spent his last years in seclusion at Blois, where he gathered a circle of poets· at his court. He was himself a poet of very great mastery (though of quite a different stamp from the disreputable and original Villon), and I very much regret being unable to render some of his Ballades (such as the marvellous 'Le beau soleil, le jour saint Valentin ... ') into English verse.

Queen Blanche[4] who had a siren's voice,
white as a lily on the plain;
Big-footed Bertha, by Heaven's choice
mother of great Charlemagne;
and Joan-of-Arc from proud Lorraine
the English burned from cruel fear -
where are they, where, O Mother of Men?
Where are the snows of yesteryear?

Don't ask, Prince,[5] in one month again,
nor yet in twelve where they all are;
I'd only give you this refrain:
where are the snows of yesteryear?

The Old Woman Longing for the Days of Her Youth
(The Lament of the 'Belle Hëaulmière')
from *The Testament* (1462)

I thought I heard the whore complain
who sold helmets as a cover-trade,
wishing the days would come again
when she was young; and this she said:-
"Old age, a cruel trick you've played!
Why have you struck me down so soon?
Who'll care now if I put paid
to a life so long past its high noon?

"You've robbed me, left me in the lurch,
taken my beauty and power away.
Businessmen, men of the Church
don't give me all they have today.
No man was born who would not pay
all that he had to get that prize
(with some misgiving, I daresay)
which even beggars now despise.

"Many a man I could have had
but turned down in my dizziness
for true love of a crafty lad

I showered with limitless largesse.
I was unfaithful once or twice -
but Christ! I loved him - love him yet.
He only gave me churlishness
and loved only what he could get.

"He could have dragged me through the mud
and trampled on me - I would still
have worshipped him. Had he drawn blood
and maimed me, I'd have done his will.
I'd be in misery until
he ordered me to kiss him. Swine!
I was nothing but his swill -
and all I can do now is whine.

"Shame and sin are all I've left
for thirty years now since he died.
And I live on, old, grey, bereft,
brooding on my prime and pride.
Now look at me - I'm shrunk and dried,
and when I see how I have changed,
ravaged now by time and tide,
the undertow leaves me deranged.

"Where is that forehead's smooth expanse,
the arched eyebrows and golden hair,
the wide-set eyes, the pretty glance
which caught the wiliest unaware;
that well-proportioned nose, that pair
of little ears, that dimpled chin,
that lovely face so clear and fair
with lips of pure vermilion?

"Those long arms, shoulders slim and straight,
fine hands, breasts small and eloquent,
hips high, smooth full, in perfect state
to enter in love's tournament;
where are the broad loins and the cunt
between each firm and rounded thigh
set like a lovely ornament
within its little herbary?

"My forehead's wrinkled now, and grey
my hair; my eyebrows droop; my eyes
are bleary now whose glance was gay
and drained men's purses with their flies.
There's none a hook-nose will entice
or ears that hang like lumps of moss;
my face is faded, dead as ice;
my chin and lips like withered pods.

"So this is human beauty's lot -
hands like claws and stumpy arms,
shoulders gnarled up in a knot -
not a trace of former charms.
Breasts and hips mere shrunken forms;
my cunt is a long-dried up spring
my thighs no more than bony worms
all mottled like a sausage-skin.

"And so we mourn the good old days,
poor old fools that we are now,
squatting by a feeble blaze
of straw, like tattered heaps of tow -
so soon aflame, so soon burned low.
Once we were so proud and gay,
beautiful from top to toe.
All flesh is heir to such decay."

In Villon's day, prostitutes in Paris were subject to much harrassment from the city authorities, and were becoming (or were replaced by) girls who gained part of their livelihood as shopkeepers, and thus had a respectable base to work from. The 'Belle Hëaulmière' (sometimes translated as 'The Beautiful Armouress') was one of these, and was among the better-known demi-mondaines in the 1390's. She became the mistress of a very wealthy and powerful man (Nicolas D'Orgemont, known as 'The Lame') who, however, became involved in a mysterious intrigue against Charles VI in 1416, was imprisoned, and died the same year. The 'Belle Hëaulmière' must also have suffered a decline in fortune, since, according to Villon, she lived with a pimp until his death around 1426. When Villon knew her, in the 1450's, she was in her eighties, as decrepit and anguished as the 'Nun' of Beare, the dried-up spring that Rodin portrayed her in bronze.

Villon's Dialogue with his Heart

Who's there? *It's me.* Who's "me"? *Your heart,*
that holds on by the merest thread;
I feel my blood ebb and my strength depart
when I see you hanging down your head
like some poor lurcher cringing in a shed.
And why is that? *Because you live too fast.*
So what? *It's I who come off worst.*
Why, you ask? I'll think about it. Let me be!
When will you start thinking? When my childhood's past.
I'll say no more. That's quite all right with me.

What do you want? To be a man of substance.
You're thirty now. No younger than a mule.
Is that still childhood? No. *Then madness*
has got hold of you. Where? By the lapel?
You know nothing. Yes I do: I can tell
the difference between flies and milk. One's white,
one's black. *Is that all?* Is that too trite
for you? I'll start again. Let's see...
You're lost! Well, I'll put up a fight.
I'll say no more. That's quite all right with me.

From all this I get sorrow, you get pain.
If you had been some poor demented fool
I might have had less reason to complain,
but good and bad you spin from the same spool.
Either your head is filled with wool
or else you like damnation more than bliss.
Well, what is your reply to this?
I'll be above it when I pass away.
God, how comforting! What wisdom and what eloquence!
I'll say no more. That's quite all right with me.

Where do these ills spring from? From ill-luck.
When Saturn packed my bag for me
he put them in. *What rubbish! You're star-struck.*
You are master, yet think yourself unfree.
Solomon has written - you can see
It in the Bible - 'Men of sense

have power over planets and their influence.'
I don't believe it. As they made me, so I'll be.
What did you say? Just my kind of sense.
I'll say no more. That's quite all right with me.

You want to live? May God give me the power!
*You must then... What? Read every hour;
be penitent.* Read what? *Philosophy -
and leave your foolish friends.* I'll see.
*Now don't forget. Don't be perverse.
Don't wait so long that things get even worse.
I'll say no more.* That's quite all right with me.

PIERRE de RONSARD (1524-1585)
from "Sonnets for Hélène"

"Je Liai d'un Filet de Soie Cramoisie..."

I bound a red silk ribbon round your wrist
the other day while we engaged in chat,
but your arm was the only captive caught -
neither heart nor fancy was impressed.

O Beauty, mistress who gives me no rest,
the scales are tipped: our struggles come to naught;
you have me, mind and body, in your net
and Love cannot bind you nor hold you fast.

Mistress, I'll speak to some old sorcerer
to seek some spell to bind your will to mine,
some magic shaft that will unite our hearts.

But no - love ensorcelled soon departs.
To be young, rich, eloquent, handsome, fine -
and not charmed verses - are love's conjurer.

'Quand Vous Serez bien Vieille ...'*

When you are very old, at evening, by the fire,
spinning wool by candlelight and winding it in skeins,
you will say in wonderment as you recite my lines:
"Ronsard admired me in the days when I was fair."

Then not one of your servants dozing gently there
hearing my name's cadence break through your low repines
but will start into wakefulness out of her dreams
and bless your name - immortalised by my desire.

I'll be underneath the ground, and a boneless shade
taking my long rest in the scented myrtle-glade,
and you'll be an old woman, nodding towards life's close,

regretting my love, and regretting your disdain.
Heed me, and live for now: this time won't come again.
Come, pluck now - today - life's so quickly-fading rose.

*This poem has been freely paraphrased by Yeats in 'When you are old and grey and full of sleep'. The only line of the original that Yeats retains - 'and bending down beside the glowing bars ...' - is the only one *not* retained in the above translation.

CHARLES BAUDELAIRE (1821-1867)
from *Les Fleurs du Mal (The Flowers of Evil)*
(second version, 1861)

Harmonie du Soir

The days are approaching, when, throbbing on its stem,
each flower offers up its incense like a prayer;
sound and perfume mingle in the soft evening air
in a melancholy dance, a slow swirling balm.

Each flower offers up its incense like a prayer.
The violin quivers like a heart that knows no calm
in a melancholy dance, a slow swirling balm,
and the sky is a huge shrine, sad and beautiful and bare.

The violin quivers like a heart that knows no calm,
a tender heart which hates the void that's vast and spare;
the sky is a huge shrine, sad and beautiful and bare,
and the sun has drowned in his own blood that's set to malm.

A tender heart which hates the void that's vast and spare
picks up the pices of the past like a shattered gem;
the sun has drowned in his own blood that's set to malm,
and like a monstrance your memory shines through my despair.

The Lid

Wheresoever he may go, upon land or on sea,
under sky of flame, or pale polar sun,
whether servant of Christ, or Aphrodite's devotee,
as resplendent as Croesus, or in brooding beggardom;

be he townsman or countryman, staying put or roaming free,
whether his poor brain be quick or be numb,
everywhere Man endures the fear of mystery
and looks above him only in a cowed delirium.

The smothering sky is like a sepulchre wall,
a ceiling lit up by an endless music-hall
where every actor walks across a blood-drenched stage;

free-thinker's terror, hope of demented sage,
the Sky! black lid of the huge casserole
in which Mankind seethes innumerably small.

Spleen *("Quand le ciel bas et lourd...")*

When, like a heavy lid, the sky, low and dark
weighs on the groaning mind beset by angst and fright;
and when, embracing the whole horizon's arc,
it pours a sombre day on us, more desolate than night -

when the earth is turned into a dripping prison-cell
where Hope, like a bat, with echo-less screams
bruises and beats its shy wings against the wall
and knocks its head upon the rotted ceiling-beams -

when, fanning out its long streaks of water, the rain
imitates the bars of an enormous gaol,
and a horde of dumb spiders creeps into my brain
to weave and weave their webs into a monstrous veil -

then, suddenly, bells swing and hurl out their din,
their horrible fury howling up on high,
like wandering spirits with neither home nor kin
beginning their relentless wailing to the sky -

and with neither drum nor music dreary hearses file
in procession through my soul: Hope, half dead,
weeps defeated; while Anguish, despotic and vile
plants his loathsome black flag upon my bowed head.

ARTHUR RIMBAUD (1854-1891)

At "The Green Man" *
5 p.m.

I'd torn my boots to shreds for seven or eight
days on the stones of the roads. At "The Green Man"
in Charleroi I ordered bread and butter and a plate
of all they had to offer: some half-cold ham.

Happily I stretched out my legs beneath the green
table. I studied the wallpaper's artless designs.
And to make it all perfect, a natural queen
of a girl with enormous teats and sparkling eyes -

(it would take more than a kiss to frighten her!)
- smilingly brought me my bread and butter there
and the lukewarm ham set on a coloured plate -

ham pink and white and flavoured with the sheer
tang of garlic - and filled up a huge mug with beer
whose froth was turned to gold by a shaft of evening light.

* (See also Appendix II)

37

The Plundered Heart

My poor heart's dribbling at the stern,
my heart covered in nicotine:
they squirt soup onto it in turn,
my poor heart's dribbling at the stern:
beneath the quipping unconcern
of sailors raucously obscene,
my poor heart's dribbling at the stern,
my heart covered in nicotine!

Ithyphallic, erkish, lewd,
their dirty jokes have tainted it!
In the wheelhouse there are crude
graffiti, ithyphallic, lewd.
O let my heart be cleansed, renewed
by wondrous waves immersing it!
Ithyphallic, erkish, lewd,
their dirty jokes have tainted it.

When they have chewed their quids to pulp,
O plundered heart, what shall I do?
Bacchic hiccups, sniggers, yelps.
When they have chewed their quids to pulp:
my guts (if I can only gulp
my heart back) will be churning, too:
when they have chewed their quids to pulp,
O plundered heart, what shall I do?

The Lice-Seekers *

When, full of red torments, the child's troubled head
entreats the white swarm of shadowy dreams,
two gentle grown-up sisters come close to his bed
with fragile fingers like silver-tipped machines.

Before a casement window they sit the child down,
a window open wide to where the azure air

bathes a tangle of flowers, and upon his tousled crown
their terrible, fine fingers move with magical care.

He listens to the sighing of their apprehensive breath
which smells of the long honeys of the flowering earth,
interrupted now and then by a subtle hiss:
saliva caught on the lip, or desire for a kiss.

He hears their dark eyelashes flicker overhead
in the sweetsmelling silence, and their sovereign fingers,
    sweet,
electric in his languidness meet
in a crackle: little lice are dead.

And there rises in him the wine of listlessness,
delirium-inducing harmonica sigh;
he feels with the slowness of each careful caress
endlessly surging and ebbing the desire to cry.

* See also Appendix I

Les Stupra
Violations

1.

The animals of old rutted even on the run,
their glans encrusted with blood and with shit.
Our ancestors displayed their organs as befit
the folds of the sheath and the scrotum's grainy dun.

Mediaeval man needed substantial gear
for a female - whether she be angel or sow;
and to judge from his breeches[1] (even to allow
for exaggeration) can't have beeen too bad an engineer.

Besides, man is equal to the very proudest beast;
we are wrong to be humbled by their genitals' great size.
But a sterile hour has struck: the gelding has no feast,

nor the bullock, in blood; and nobody will rise
to display a pride of parts with a wholesomeness long ceased
in thickets which exuberate with comic children's cries.

2.

Our buttocks are not theirs. I have seen diverse
unbuttonings behind shady hedges and banks;
and in unconstrained bathings where children splash their pranks
I've observed the design and execution of our arse.

Firmer, often paler, underneath their screen of hairs,
our rumps are striking in the contours of their flanks.
For women it is only on the parting furrow's banks
that the long tufted satin blooms for our commerce.

An ingenuity, touching and sublime
like the faces of angels in icons, imitates
the cheek which hollows a smile incarnadine.

O that we were naked too! seeking joy that satiates,
facing our companion's finest part in its prime,
both free to murmur sobs as our happiness dictates?

3.

Dark and wrinkling like a purpled pink
it humbly pants in moss still damp with love
that followed the soft slope to where the buttocks clove,
to where white buttocks led to its flesh-hem's brink.[2]

Filaments have wept like tears of milk
in the cruel south wind which has driven them back
through clots of red marl, to be lost along the track
where the slope called them with surfaces of silk.

My dream has often kissed its enchanted orifice;
my soul, in jealousy of carnal intercourse,
has made this its tear-bottle and its nest of sobs.

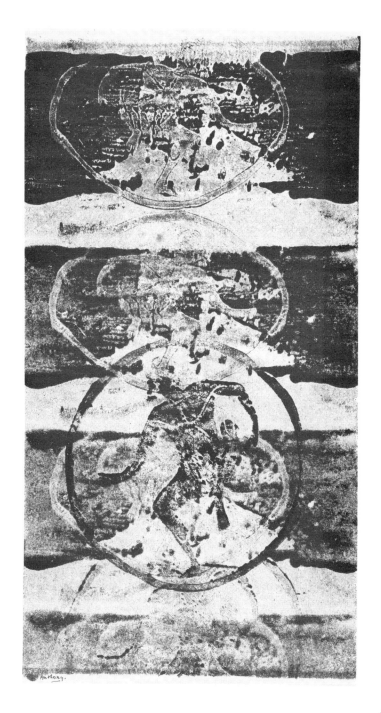

41

It is the rapturous olive and the wheedling flute that calls,
the tube from which the heavenly praline falls,
feminine Canaan that dew anoints and orbs.

[1] In the seventh line of number 1, between 'breeches' and 'even', the name
'Kléber' occurs in the original, referring presumably to a portrait of the
stonemason's son from Strasbourg who rose to become a great Revolutionary
general and served brilliantly under Napoleon in Egypt. I have, for clarity's
sake, omitted the reference, obscure to English-speaking readers, since the
sense of the verse as a whole is not thereby significantly altered.

[2] In the fourth line of number 3, the French reads *au bord de son ourlet'*,
which Oliver Bernard in his literal translation (Penguin Books) renders as 'at
its crater's edge'. *'Ourlet'* can mean 'crater-rim', 'the rim of the ear', or 'hem',
and Rimbaud obviously intends all three meanings to merge.

The Poor at Church

Penned between oak pews in corners of the church
which their stinking breath heats up, every sorry eye
on the chancel dripping gilt, and the choir in their perch
with their twenty jowls yowling pious hymns to the sky.

Sniffing in the smell of wax as if it were bread,
happy and humbled, just like beaten dogs,
the poor offer up to God prayers from feet like lead,
the stubborn and ridiculous *oremus*es in clogs.

For the women it's relief to wear the benches smooth
after six dreary days which God has made them bear.
They comfort children-like creatures swathed in shawls, and soothe
the infants who cry as if they'd die so soon from care.

With unwashed breasts exposed these eaters of soup
with a prayer in their eyes, but never a prayer
watch hoydens showing off in an impudent group
with hats all awry before the women's stare.

42

Outside - the cold and the hunger and the men on the booze;
ah well! Another hour to go - then unspeakable trial.
An assortment of old dewlapped women all the while
are whimpering and whispering and sniffling in their pews

- these are the frightened and the epileptic ones
whom you avoided yesterday off the boulevards;
and nuzzling ancient missals, sightless as stones
are the blind whom dogs lead into bleak backyards.

And all of them, dribbling a grovelling stupid faith,
recite their unending complaint to Jesus
who dreams above, glass-yellow, like a wraith
far from wicked men, this, or fat as cheeses,

far from the smell of mouldy clothes and meat,
and the repulsive gestures of the overplayed black farce.
And as the prayer blossoms with full poetic force
and the mysteries become more mystic and more sweet,

from where the sunlight is dying in the aisles,
with shallow folds of silk and pale green smiles
the more distinguished ladies - Christ, with suffering livers! -
    droop
their long yellow fingers in the holy-water stoup.

Squattings

Very late, when he feels his stomach start to churn,
Brother Milotus, one eye on the skylight pane
where the sun polished bright as a pan has returned
to make him dizzy and send him a migraine,
under the sheets gives his priestly form a turn.

He struggles underneath the blanket's dirty fluff
and gets out of bed, knees to trembling chest,
as flustered as an old man who has swallowed his snuff
because he has to gather up his nightshirt round his waist
while holding up a pot for his arse's autograph.

43

Now he's squatting, chilly, with curled-up toes
and chattering teeth beneath the window-sash
where the sun daubs the paper panes with cake-yellow hues.
And snuffling in the rays like a coral reef of flesh
is the incandescent crimson of the old man's nose.

*   *   *   *

He simmers at the fire with twisted arms,
blubber lip on his belly. He feels his thighs slip
into the flames, and as he squirms
in scorching breeches, feeling his pipe
go out, something like a bird stirs through the alarms
in a belly serene as a mountain of tripe.

Round about him a jumble of furniture rests
on dirty stomachs among grimy rags.
Stools like weird toads are piled in strange incests,
cupboards with mouths like choirmasters sag
and yawn with a lassitude full of loathsome lusts.

The narrow room is filled with the sickening heat
and rags stuff themselves in the old man's brain.
He listens to the hairs growing in his sweating skin,
and sometimes, loudly hiccuping, he moves away again
knocking down his crippled stool as he makes his retreat.

*   *   *   *

And in the evening by the moonlight which drops
dribblings of light on the contours of his arse,
against a background of pink snow like hollyhocks
squats a shadow with details dim and diverse.
A fantastic nose follows Venus among the sky's dark blots.

*   *   *   *

Vowels

A black, E white, I red, U green, O blue: vowels
I will tell you your secret origins some day.
A - black bodice of flies, the glittering inlay
that buzzes in the stench of ripped-out bowels;

gulfs of shadow. E - whitenesses of mists and tents,
iceberg spears, white kings, tall trembling cow-parsnips.
I - purples, spat blood, the smile of beautiful lips
in anger, or the ecstasies of penitents.

U - cycles, divine undulations of viridian seas,
peace of pastures dotted with animals, the peace
of furrows wrought by alchemy on foreheads of the wise.

O - supreme Trumpet full of strange piercing notes,
and silences traversed by Worlds and Angel Hosts:
O, the Omega, violet beam of Her Eyes.

"O Castles, O Seasons!"*

O castles, O seasons!
What heart has not its treasons?

I pursued the magic lore
of happiness none can ignore.

May it flourish, every morning
the Gallic cock crows his warning.

Ah! I'll never want again:
it has taken me in train.

Body and soul enchanted,
my efforts dissipated.

O castles, O seasons!

Alas, the hour of its release
will be the hour of my decease.

O castles, O seasons!

* (The difficulties involved in translating Rimbaud's poetry are discussed in Appendix II.)

From the Danish

CARL BAGGE (1938 -)
from *poems 1962-1964* **(unpublished)**

Has Died

Has died
was one of
was born
was one of
to the last
who was
who came to
who became
and who was
if he had
and was
and was
that was
it was
was not
so very
who was
but will
it came
all who
who had
always
so faithful

and the children.

These Storks are Here to be Seen

There are storks
here you certainly
know it you hear them chatter
        and bicker
        and flutter
        and jabber
        and jostle
        and babble
        and cackle
        and cuddle
        and chortle
You build a sanctuary
and ask them to move, please.
Ask them to be a little quieter

if they will.

Hunger

He: I am a fly.
I cannot fly.
My wings are dissolving.
Flower, lend me new ones.

She: I am a flower.
You may borrow my leaves.
I am called Butterwort.
I am hungry.

Both: I knew
you would come
and fill me with joy.

He: I am happy.

She: I am hungry.

He: I was happy before.
I danced all day.
I sucked nectar
all day.

She: I love to see you,
your fat body,
your immobility.
I am hungry.

Both: I knew
you would come
and fill me with joy.

He: I am happy.	*She:* I am hungry.

He: I was a fly.	*She:* Your legs will shrivel.
I cannot fly.	I will grow,
My wings are dissolving.	devouring slowly.
Flower, lend me new ones.	I am hungry.

> *Both:* I knew
> you would come
> and fill me with joy.

She: I am hungry.

Thirst

To create
relieving
is to love oneself admiring
believing
that one's vital worth can
satiate
others' desiring.

It is Night

It is night and you are sleeping,
I will smile happy and hushed;
your dreams are in your keeping
while I draw upon your breast.

I will doodle wicked men
who pluck children from your breast
and plant violets around them
to satisfy their raging thirst.

You will weep while they are drinking
while they drain your life away.

They will sing while you are sinking
a soft, forgotten lay.

You will smile; your hidden dreams
I'll interpret on your breast.
Who will teach your softened limbs
to swim before the day has burst?

Your floating freckles I will number
when the sun is blazing full.
I will waken from my slumber
clinging to a doodled soul.

Enormous Bulls

Enormous bulls
safe in bottles
make men seem superior
and cows equal
through calf-stencils
in Christian comfort.

TOVE DITLEVSEN (1918-   )

Recognition
from *Pigesind (A Girl's Mind)* (1939)

We two must never, never more must part
- listen to what I'm telling you, my dear.
Our happiness is so great that you must know
there is a limit to what I can bear.

At home we used to have a vase
which I was not allowed to touch at all.
It was big and heavy, elaborately decorated
with rosebuds that were delicate and small.

And only because it was so wild and daring,
in all the tension that a forbidden thing will germ
I took down the vase one morning
and felt between my hands its noble form.

Strange fancies flashed across my mind -
it was so big and heavy, I so small.
To smash it was wicked and unthinkable,
but I was scared because I wanted it to fall.

For eternally-excited moments
I stood and struggled with the evil voice
that whispered: *Do something really dangerous
now that you're alone and have the chance.*

And powerful forces compelled me to let go.
Now the world is pain and without joy.
Ten thousand pieces can never be united
and the good angels turn their backs to cry.

I want you to know me, and to know
that what is carefully entrusted me will slip away.
And therefore, for the sake of our great happiness
please, please don't think too much of me.

Eternal Triangle
from *Little Verden (Small World)* **(1942)**

There are two men in the world
who constantly cross my way;
one of them is he whom I love,
the other one loves me.

The first is in a nightly dream
within my dark, dark soul.
The other one stands at the door of my heart
and never will cross the sill.

The first gave me a springtime breath
of joy that soon was gone.
The second gave me all his life
and got not an hour in return.

The first one streams in the song of my blood
where loving is true and free.
The other is one with the sorry day
where dreams are drowned in me.

Each woman stands between these two:
in love, beloved and pure.
And it may happen they fuse into one
once in a hundred years.

GRETHE RISBJERG THOMSEN (1925-)

The Word
from *Havet og Stjernen (The Sea and the Star)* **(1959)**

My fear is a fear of the perfect, the polished and shining.
My dread is a strange kind of dread that's hard to explain.
I'm afraid of the danger that lurks in all tidy thinking:
stunted by neatly-trimmed patterns life struggles in vain.

I'm frightened of words that are ready and rigid and hollow,
that put the world barren and bound in a frame.
And still I have caught each faltering gladness and sorrow
in the net of my words while my heart was quite without flame.

I search for the words that are living and naked and timid,
the poor ones that become rich in hearts that resound.
What can we do with all the fine songs that are frigid?
I dream about poems as free as wings or as wind.

I search for the vague, drifting poems that are not poems,
just tidings, simple and fresh from a secret domain;
just messages coming from something we dare not abandon,
our deepest dream that alone is not fleeting and vain.

One Night, Perhaps a March Night
from *Dagen og Natten (Day and Night)* (1948)

With every passing moment
I die a little bit.
I carry death within me
through every year I live.

One night, perhaps a March night
mild with rain and mist,
I'll walk into the darkness
and let the dying rest.

BIRTHE ARNBAK (1923 -)

Country Lass Unveiled*
from *Skjulesteder (Hiding Places)* (1955)

With a clean conscience and dirty feet
I went to meet
my true love while the birds sang
from tree to tree
a last time.

But when next morning I passed by
the tree that God had lived inside
when I was still a child
He came out -
"YOU!" he said -

*'Veiled Country Lass' (*Bondepige med Slør*) is a Danish pudding of apples,
rye-breadcrumbs and whipped cream.

"Where did you go BARE-LEGGED last night?"
and held me by my plait,
and pointed with an angry look
at my feet -
"Shame on you!"

VIGGO STUCKENBERG (1863-1905)

Snow
from a collection of anti-Fairy Tales, *The Dragon's Heart and Other Stories* (1899)

It is a long way, a long way away in the land where all the Fairy Tales happen.

Out on a flat, snow-covered, endless, barren field stands a tumbledown hut, and in the hut's only room sits a bent old man breathing on the ice on the window-pane and staring out over the lonely snow-plain which is empty, cold and trackless, white and without life all the way to the frost-blue clouds on the horizon. The old man's breath spreads like thick steam over the pane. The frost creaks in the woodwork; the cold steals in from outside through cracks and chinks, and long icicles hang down from the eaves like a lattice over the window.

The old man does not move; he scarcely blinks his eyes, so fixedly does he stare out towards the horizon. Farthest out there, where the flat white snowfield draws a straight horizon-line with the darkling sky, it runs down like the edge of a sea that rolls wave after wave, slowly and endlessly along a shore.

It is mankind's youth going to the Castle where the Princess and half the Kingdom are to be won.

The old man stretches his hands towards the cold window, and presses his forehead against the ice-covered pane; and his mouth quivers as if he is speaking. But no sound escapes his lips. He is as dumb as one whose soul bears a sorrow no-one and nothing can alleviate. His gaze is as fixed and tearless as in one who sees life withered and wasted, and can do nothing. Only his brain is alive - it struggles desperately and monotonously with ever the same useless, futile thought: to stop that host.

But even if he shouted they would not hear him. His voice would sound like a bird crying above their heads, and no-one would see him.

For out there on the horizon where they walk, the white snow-field looks like a meadow decked with daisies and bindweed, and his house looks like a jasmine-smothered abode of kisses and embraces and dreams; and the winter sky's cold heavy clouds like summer's clearest air. And the dead stillness of the frost on the white fields sounds like the song of unseen larks. It is green and fertile and blossoming all around; and far in front lies the Castle with the Princess and half the Kingdom like a song upon the lips.

Day in and day out the old man sits and stares. The crowd never stops, and no-one ever rides to the Castle. But round about him he sees only barren fields and lonely huts, huts that stand empty and waiting, and huts where old men sit like he does, staring out of frozen panes into a changeless Winter, always the same, cold and white, like a memory of what is dead for ever, out into that Winter which is the Dragon slowly swallowing those who never won the Princess.

NOTE: Viggo Stuckenberg's small collection of short anti-Fairy Tales has the Danish title of '*Vejbred*', which means 'plantain', a widespread wayside plant, whose name in Danish can be translated literally as 'way-broad', and whose English dialect name is Waybread. The eighteen tales comprising '*Vejbred*' were translated into English and published under the title of 'B*y the Wayside*' in 1917. 'Snow' is included in a new translation entitled '*The Dragon's Heart and Other Stories*', not yet published.

From the Swedish

LARS HULDÉN (1926-   )

from *Enrönnen* (1966)*

1.

The author has today
invented fourteen striking phrases
six metaphors
and two Homeric similes.

He goes out to his wife in the kitchen
and tells her of his inventions
and gets a pat on the cheek.

Not only does he
give his readers opportunity
to say Oh and smile

he has today also
enriched literary research
by fourteen striking phrases, etc.

2.

How sweet it is to be
a well-respected man!
How sweet that I can meet
and smile with other men.

Enrönnen, 'The Lone Rowan', is a common Swedish place-name in Professor
Huldén's native south-west Finland.

O all who are respectable,
how confidingly you gaze
into each others' eyes
and nod when you meet!

Behold! all that you have done
has been rather good.
Pray do continue
as you have begun.

Verily I say
unto you: None
shall I take with me today
out of Paradise.

3.

The lone rowan-tree
on its rock
wrestles with the wind.

I won't let you go.
Not until...

And see
this year a bunch
of red rowanberries
on the southern side.

4.

Now it was the Morn of Glory.
While I slowly wakened up
I knew all the time that Now
You Are Waking Up Lad To
The Morn Of Glory.

The hum of insects was the first thing
a rising falling organ tone
MMMMnnnnMMMMnnnn
over currant bushes in which I
later was to stand.

Out on the meadow sunwarm and no wind
and the grass dewfresh as it shall be
on The Morn Of Glory.

I walked in my white shirt.
Quick snakes ran about and
tickled the tops of my toes.

I was ill from laughing
on The Mohorn Of Glohory.

Nearby I saw other white shirts.
Come! I heard vaguely. Now let us
sing a tra-la.

Then I just sat down and enjoyed it all.

5.

My love follow me
follow me to Morven.
There we shall, we

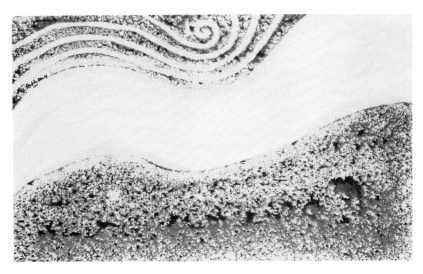

shall take our homespun breeches off,
take them off on the moor
and make a fire,

make a turf-fire and love,
make love together every morning,
morning in Morven.

6.

My first love was called Fordson M 22.
I remember our first meeting, his rumbling
bass, the bright smoke
over field and wood.

His starting handle hung
and swung between his front wheels.

I went forward, took it gently
in my hand - it was so unyielding.
I cranked and cranked and
myself became unyielding and strong.

7.

Your poem will be
about impossible and unimaginable
but incontestable
love.

Your words will be
like birds that
veer away from smoke and the
uniformity of towns.

Only the most watchful
who morning after morning
come to the birch-hut will hear
your true song.

8.

The strict morality of dogs
permits no deliveries
from unfriendly vehicles, especially
at night when citizens have to sleep.

Equally-little approved are wearers
of clothes that deviate from accepted
norms: do not for example go out
on the road in evening dress
before 6 p.m.

It is also forbidden for pedestrians
to look thoughtful.
If the dog's friends
happen to be playing in the churchyard

during a burial
and the deceased starts
coughing in the coffin - what a row!
Morality demands that corpses be dead.

9. **Clown Cleppo**

Clown Cleppo laughs
and everybody laughs.

Clown Cleppo cries
and everybody laughs.

Clown Cleppo screams
and everybody laughs.

Clown Cleppo shuffles out
and everybody shuffles out.

10.

Jump! they all shouted.
And look at your mother.

All right, I said.
Here's where I come to Mummy.

She's going to give me a big hug.
Mother Earth.

Mr Wolf!
from *Herr Varg! (Mr Wolf!)* (1969)

I have consistently maintained,
Mr Wolf, that you should be
designated for conservation!

? ?

What do you mean by
staring at me with those
wild eyes?

? ?

You should show your gratitude
now that you know what I have done for you
and for all wolves.

? ?

Between ourselves, it is only
a matter of time before you are protected
all year round.

? ?

Well, off with you now -
Mr Wolf? The forest is full
of food!

? ?

You always were obstinate!
Stop staring
and growling, I say!
Just think about what I have told you

? ?

How nice I have been
to you and your children, Mr Wolf!
Let me pass!

? ?

There's surely nothing wrong in
being human when one is
as well-disposed as I am?

! !

Mr Wolf! Wolf! Wo-
Aoorgh puuisch......

From the German

BERTOLT BRECHT (1898-1956)

Concerning a Drowned Girl
from *Die Hauspostille* (1927)

When she was drowned and floated down
to the larger rivers from the smaller streams
marvellously Heaven's opal shone
as if it felt it had to make amends.

Algae clung to her body, and weed,
so that she slowly became much heavier.
Fish swam coldly round her feet;
even on her last journey plants and animals impeded her.

And the sky in the evening became dark as smoke
and held the day in suspension by the stars at night,
but soon again dawn broke
so that for her there would still be darkness and light.

While her pale body was rotting in the water -
first her face, then her hands, and finally her hair,
it happened (just as slowly) that God gradually forgot her.
Then she became carrion in the rivers with all the carrion there.

Surabaya Johnny[*]

from *Happy End* (1929)

(to music by Kurt Weill)

1.

I was young - God, only sixteen.
You came up from Burma one night.
You said I must go away with you,
you'd look after things, see me right.
I asked what you did for a living -
So help me God! you said to me
that you'd something to do with the railway
and nothing to do with the sea.
You said so much, Johnny.   *from the very start, Johnny,*
Not a word was true, Johnny, *you shot me a line.*
I hate you so much, Johnny,
as you stand there grinning
- take that pipe out of your gob, you swine!

Surabaya-Johnny, why are you such a brute?
Surabaya-Johnny, my God, how much I love you!
Surabaya-Johnny, why do I feel so blue?
You have no heart, Johnny, and I love you, I do.

2.

At first every day was like Sunday
- until I went off with you.
But then after only a fortnight
there was nothing right I could do.
Up and down through the Punjab,
along the river down to the sea...
A face that looks about forty
stares back from the mirror at me.
It wasn't love you wanted, Johnny.
You wanted cash, Johnny.
But I only looked, Johnny, at your mouth's red line.
You asked for everything, Johnny.

[*]Surabaya is a port in North East Java.

I gave you more, Johnny
- take that pipe out of your gob, you swine!

Surabaya-Johnny, why are you such a brute?
Surabaya-Johnny, my God, how much I love you!
Surabaya-Johnny, why do I feel so blue?
You have no heart, Johnny, and I love you, I do.

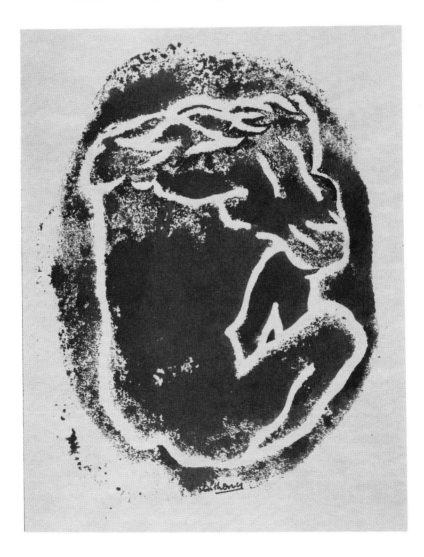

3.

I never really wondered
why you had that name.
But up and down the coastline
you had a certain fame.
In a sixpenny bed one morning
I will hear the roar of the sea,
and you'll leave without any warning
and your ship will be in at the quay.
You have no heart, Johnny.
You're a bum, Johnny.
You're leaving me, Johnny - tell me why.
I love you in spite of all, Johnny,
like the very first day, Johnny
- take that pipe out of your gob you swine!

Surabaya-Johnny, why are you such a brute?
Surabaya-Johnny, my God, how much I love you!
Surabaya-Johnny, why do I feel so blue?
You have no heart, Johnny, and I love you - I do!

Ballad of the Jew-Lover Marie Sanders
from *The Round Heads and the Pointed Heads* (1938)
(to music by Hanns Eisler)

In Nuremberg they issued a decree
which many a woman wept over, who
lay in bed with the wrong man.

"The price of meat's gone up in the suburbs.
They are beating the drums of hate.
God in Heaven, if they're going to do something
let it be tonight!"

Marie Sanders, your lover's
hair is just a shade too black.
You'd better not see him again,
the one you were with last night.

"The price of meat's gone up in the suburbs.
They are beating the drums of hate.
God in Heaven, if they're going to do something
let it be tonight!"

Mother, give me the key.
It's not as bad as all that.
And the moon's still shining...

"The price of meat's gone up in the suburbs.
They are beating the drums of hate.
God in Heaven, if they're going to do something
let it be tonight!"

One morning in the small hours
she went through the town
in her nightshirt, with a notice hung beneath
her shaven head. The mob howled. She looked calm.

"The price of meat's gone up in the suburbs.
The homeless are saying tonight:
'O God, if we had only listened
we would have foreseen our plight!' "

For 'Whore's Song' ('*Lied eines Freudenmädchens*'), also from *The Round Heads and the Pointed Heads*, see Appendix III.

The Ballad of the Lady and the Forester
from *Herr Puntila and his Squire Matti* (1948)
(to music by Paul Dessau)

There once lived a Lady in Sweden's gold land
and fair and lovely was she.
"O Forester mine, my garter's undone,
is undone, is undone -
Forester, bend down and tie it for me."

"O Lady, O Lady, don't look at me so.
I serve you to bind soul to breath.
Your breasts they are white, but my hatchet is cold,
it is cold, it is cold.
Love is a sweet thing, but bitter is death."

The Forester fled that very same night
and rode to the edge of the sea.
"O Captain, O Captain, take me in your boat,
in your boat, in your boat -
Captain, I have to cross over the sea."

A vixen she once fell in love with a cock:
"O Golden Bird, don't you love me?"
And fine was the evening, but when came the dawn,
came the dawn, came the dawn,
all the cock's feathers swirled under the tree.

Elephant Song
from *The Good Woman of Sezuan* (1942)
(to music by Paul Dessau)

Seven Elephants had Mr Chin
and then there was the eighth one.
Seven were wild and the eighth was tame
and the eighth was appointed foreman.
Trot faster!
Trot faster!
This forest's for the plough.
It must be cleared before night falls
and it's almost night time now.

Seven elephants cleared the trees away
and Mr Chin rode high on the eighth one.
All day long number eight stood idly on guard
and observed how much they dragged behind them.
Dig faster!
Dig faster!
This forest's for the plough.

It must be cleared before night falls
and it's almost night time now.

Seven elephants wanted no more -
they had had enough of tree-clearing.
Mr Chin was afraid that the seven would renegue
and he gave a sack of rice to the eighth one.
What's behind it?
What's behind it?
This forest's for the plough.
It must be cleared before night falls
and it's almost night time now.

Seven elephants had no tusks.
The only tusks were on the eighth one.
Number eight was the gaffer while they wore themselves out
and the boss was weak from laughing.
Dig harder!
Dig harder!
This forest's for the plough.
It must be cleared before night falls
and it's almost night time now.

Lisongo Poems

SOMBO MONOKO (1941-)
(Unpublished)

Sombo Monoko ('old monkey-mouth') is an ironic pseudonym of the remarkable Binga (properly Mbenga) Pygmoid who told these poems—which are not traditional in form or content. MBENGA (Bambenga, Bamphenga or Baiinga) is a general name for different Pygmoid groups—including Mbenzele and Ngombe—in the southern border area of the Central African Republic and adjoining parts of the Congo People's Republic and Cameroun, none of whom have a language of their own, but speak the languages of the different 'Negro' groups (Bantu—and Sudanic—speaking) who outnumber them and include the Bantu-speaking language groups Lisongo (more properly Mbati), Mpyemo, Pomo and Pande, and the Sudanic-speaking Ngbaka. The Lisongo (Mbati) and Ngbaka moved westwards over the Ubangi river to the south-eastern part of the Central African Republic around Mbaïki at the beginning of the last century, and at the beginning of the present one were still hunters like the Binga—though much less effective, for the Binga whom they 'owned' hunted for them.

The teller of these impromptu 'poems' is acutely aware of the great and terrible changes that have occurred—and continue to occur—among the peoples who used to hunt in a forest which now largely cleared. Some Binga are crane-drivers for concession-companies which are cutting down the forest, while others remain the traditional and ostensible—but, by our standards, unbelievably free—'servants' of taller village 'masters', and continue to hunt the diminishing game and gather in the forest.

Life

The darkness is
The darkness is good
The Forest is good
to its hunters.

Song

I am standing
naked by the pool
with the moon
admiring its full
reflection in the full water,
making love
to the moon
in the moonlight.

The monkeys
have stopped screaming
where I passed by,
and everything
is silent as the moon
as the moon and I
make love,
save for the sound
of moon-scattering
water I dive into
after little
monkey-cries
of fitness.

'Tamba Bulé'[1]

I knew in the Forest
I knew clearly
where all understood.
But where everything
is without understanding
I do not know.

I knew in the Forest
where I was lord of bees and antelope;
but where everything is secret and the same
I do not know
and I am 'to do'.

When I was 'I am'
I knew in the Forest.

Song About Questions

A white man has come
to monkey-mouth
asking questions.
- Do I play the musical bow[2]

that catches music like a snare?
- Do I play the musical bow?
Heeee!
- Will I sing a song for him?
- How long a walk to Ndongo?
- Do I play the *Molorou*?[3]
Heee!
Heee!
Asking questions,
white man,
not like the Fathers,
wearing what we wear.[4]
White man,
pale as the moon
you come, you go,
far away, like the moon.
Will you sing me your song,
white man? Do you
play the *Molorou*?
How long a walk to your village?
Maybe I'll teach you to play
or shoot with the bow.
But we are sick,
white man.
My child is sick,
and the Forest is running away.
My child is sick, white man.
Why is he sick?
I'll sing you a song,
white man,
a song for the moon,
a song about plantains,
a song about the musical bow
that catches music like a snare.
Heeya! Heeyaaaa!
Heeya! Heeyaa-heee![5]
Heeya! Aaahee-yaaaa!
Heeyaaa-hee! Heeya!
Aaahee-yaaa-hee!
But first
buy me some palm-wine,

moon-skin, and give me a smoke
and tell me,
monkey-mouth,
why are there questions?

1. I have given a title to this poem a phrase in the Ngwana language, one of
those spoken by the Mbuti Pygmies of north-eastern Zaïre, which means,
literally, 'walking empty'.
2. The musical bow, a small hunting bow tapped with a stick while the open
mouth acts as a resonator - a sort of large Jaw (or 'Jew's') Harp - is a Pygmy
musical instrument used also by non-Pygmies. It symbolises the snare, and is
used on hunting songs.
3. The *Molorou* or *Koundi* is a five-stringed musical instrument shaped some-
thing like a boat, and sounding rather like a harp.
4. Pygmies and Pygmoids wear a simple breech-clout made either from bark-
cloth or cotton remnants. It is much despised by non-Pygmies.
5. The Binga yodel a great deal, and their songs often consist of a rich,
polyphonic yodelling.

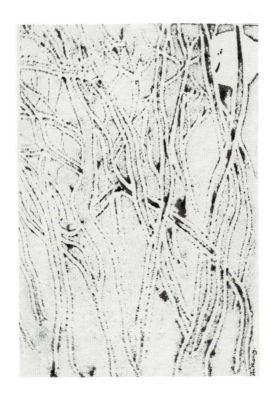

Mesopotamian Poems

Sumer, the land of Kish, Nippur, Babylon and Ur, though by no means the home of the first civilization, nevertheless saw the early rise of rival city-states which grew out of the fertile land around the Tigris and Euphrates. The Sumerians probably were conquerors from the North, who, arriving during the fourth millennium BC or later, quickly irrigated the land and built the greedy cities, which depended on it before being conquered in turn by Semitic tribes in the course of the third millennium. Being the first literate inhabitants of the area, their influence pervaded the civilizations which succeeded them; and, like the language of the Romans in medieval Europe, the Sumerian tongue and script were used centuries after power had passed to the Semitic Assyrians. Early texts of the famous *Epic of Gilgamesh* were written in the learned, priestly jargon of Sumerian.

Much of the cosmogony of the Sumerians was shared by Assyrians, Hittites, Palestinians, Syrians, Israelites and early Greeks. The names of the city-states have survived with a strong resonance, through the medium of the Bible.

The Sumerian City of Paradise*

It is for you, the land of Dilmun.
The land of Dilmun is pure.
It is a pure place, and it is for you.
The land of Dilmun is pure and clean.
The land of Dilmun is clean.
The land of Dilmun is bright.
In Dilmun they lay down together alone.
Where Enki lay with his wife is clean;
that place is bright,
where Enki lay with his wife.
In Dilmun there was no crow to croak.
There was no speckled bird of death to cry death.
The lion did not devour,
nor did the wolf carry off the lamb.
Wild beasts did not eat the corn,
and the dove did not mourn.
Eye-disease did not say "I am eye-disease", for there was none.
Headache did not say "I am headache", for there was none.
Old women did not say "I am an old woman", for there was none.

Old men did not say "I am an old man", for there was none.
No girl who had not become a woman was given in marriage.
No man commanded the course of the canal to be altered.
No prince turned away his side.
No man said "The liar lies".
Beside the city no-one lamented.

*The Sumerian isle of the blessed was situated where the two rivers flowed into the Arabian Gulf, and it was reserved, not for the ordinary dead, but for the heroes. It was called Dilmun, and may actually be the island of Bahrain. It is the subject of a unique Sumerian myth concerning Enki (the Water God) and Ninhursag (the Earth Mother). The only imperfection in Dilmun is its lack of water - and this Enki provides. On Ninhursag Enki begets Ninsar or Ninsu, the goddess of plants; on her he begets other vegetation goddesses, and so on, until eventually eight plants are begotten - which Enki devours before Ninhursag can give them names. (The giving of names being, of course, a very important thing to a great many peoples.) Ninhursag utters a terrible curse on Enki, and he is stricken with illness in eight parts of his body. Ninhursag is persuaded by a crafty fox to cure Enki's sickness, and this she does by creating eight gods, one for each part of Enki's body afflicted, who duly cure him.

Inanna and Dumuzi (Ishtar and Tammuz)

Dumuzi (or Tammuz) is the prototype of all the vegetation gods who die and rise again with the spring (Adonis, Osiris, Balder, Bran) and who, like the Irish Diarmuid, was killed by a boar. Inanna is Ishtar and Astarte and the Cailleach Bhéarra, a terrible and beautiful goddess of war and love.

Uruk (Biblical Erech), now Warka, was an important southern Mesopotamian city, where Inanna had her chief temple and whose early kings used the name 'Dumuzi' as a title (like 'Minos' or 'Pharaoh') and were to some extent at least identified with the god.

The Queen of Heaven raises her bitter cry for her husband
"How long?" she cries out, for her husband.
The Queen of E-anna cries out for her husband.
The Queen of Uruk cries out for her husband.
The Queen of Hallab cries out for her husband.
Alas for her husband! Alas for her son!
Alas for her temple! Alas for her city!
For her husband who is fallen, for her son who is fallen;
for her husband who is dead, for her son who is dead;
for her husband who was taken to Uruk, who is fallen,
who was taken to Uruk and to Kullab, who is dead!
The water of Eridu is not poured out.
The shrine of Enki is not worshipped.
The mother Inanna, Queen of Heaven, laments
for her son who does not come,
for her maidens in her city who spin no more,
for her men in her city who thresh the grain no more,
for her mighty warriors who are strong no more,
for her eunuch-priests in her city who wield the knife no more.
The Queen of Heaven laments bitterly for her young consort:
"When my husband, my good husband was taken from me;
when my son, my good son was taken from me,
my husband, the early plants, died;
my son, the later plants, died.
My husband has gone to find the plants
and the plants shall return.
My son has gone to find the water
and the water shall be sweet.
My consort, like a broken pillar -
do not go forth from the city!
Exalted one, like a withered plant - do not leave the city!"

Incantation Against Headache

Enki, Lord of the Whole Earth, whose temple in Eridu (across the river from modern Basra) was called Abzu (The Abyss of Primaeval Waters under the Earth), is Water, especially in its beneficial aspect, and god of Wisdom. Obviously in Mesopotamia water is much more important than mere earth.

Utu was the kindly and gentle Sun god (Shamash in Assyrian: the Arabic for 'sun' is still 'shams') and brother to the beautiful but terrible Inanna (Ishtar).

Marduk was the local god of little Babylon; but when Babylon became the great under the Semitic Assyrian dynasty (of which Hammurabi was the third), Marduk rose in importance as a hero-god like Odin, to challenge the established gods of the older Sumerian cities, Nippur, Eridu and Uruk.)

Headache swoops over the plain, it speeds like a gale,
it flashes like lightning, it pervades everywhere,
above and below.
It has severed like a reed the man who fears no god.
It has pierced his strength like a henna-reed.
It has struck the man who is not protected by Inanna.
Glittering like a star, it has come like a flood in the
    night.
It falls upon tormented mortals, like a storm it hurls
    them down.
It has killed one.
Another runs about like one whose heart is stricken.
He is beside himself like one whose heart
    is gone out of him.
He is seared like one cast in the fire.
A mist films his eyes like a wild ass of the plain.
In his life he burns himself up, with death he is bound.
Headache is like a cyclone - no-one knows its path,
nor the sign and spell to end it.
Marduk has seen it.
He went to his father Enki's house and said:
"My father, headache has swooped over the plain,
it has sped like a gale,
and no man knows the ritual to ease the pain."
Enki replied:
"My son, what do you not know? What can I add to
    your knowledge?
What I know, you know also.

Go, Marduk my son,
to the wild cucumber which grows upon the plain.
At sunset cover your head,
and cover the wild cucumber, and encircle it with meal;
and at dawn, before the sun is risen,
uproot it.
Cut off its root. Pull out a hair
of a she-kid that has not been mounted,
and bind them both to the head of the man afflicted.
Bind the neck of the afflicted man.
Let the headache come out of his body like water.
Let it fly away like stubble borne upon the wind,
never to return.
May it be done in the name of heaven.
May it be done in the name of earth."

The Pride of Hammurabi

The Babylonian king Hammurabi (1728-1686 BC) is celebrated by the 6½ metre high basalt stele on which are engraved 300 paragraphs of a legal codex, written in Akkadian. The laws - penal, civil and commercial - were designed for the newly-founded empire which included the whole of Babylonia and Syria.

I am Hammurabi, mighty king,
king of Babylon, king of the four corners
of the earth, the king whose deeds
fill Utu's and Marduk's hearts with joy.
I raised the wall of Sippar
like a mountain of earth.
I made a marsh to surround it.
I dug out the Euphrates up to Sippar.
I raised a dyke to defend
Sippar and Babylon.
I haves made them peaceful forever.
I am Hammurabi, favourite of Utu
and beloved of Marduk.
I have done what kings of old never did.
I have built mightily for Utu my king.

Nûr-Adad

Mighty Nûr-adad
nourisher of Ur,
king of Larsa,
priest who purified
E-barra's shrine,
established in Larsa
a reign of justice
long after Eridu
had been destroyed.
And his command established
a temple as fit dwelling
for the Earth-lord Enki,
and restored the place
of Enki's ancient Kiskanu tree.

Appendix I: Comparisons

From The French

Ladies Looking for Lice
*Arthur Rimbaud (translated by X J Kennedy)**

When the child's forehead is afire with red
Tortures and he longs for vague white dreams to come,
Two enchantress big sisters steal close to his bed
With tinselly fingers, nails of platinum.

By a casement thrown open they sit the child down
Where blue air bathes stealthily the budded stalk
And in his locks thick with dew and along his crown
Their sorceress hands thin and terrible walk.

He traces the song of their hesitant breath,
Spumed honey that feels forth slow tendrils, the hiss
That now and then breaks it: spit blown through the teeth
And sucked back on the lips, or desire for a kiss.

He hears their black lashes beat through the perfume
Of the quiet and a crackle like static: the slice
Of their fingernails, queens of indolent gloom,
Passing death sentences on little lice.

Now in him a wine mounts: Laziness,
Sound that can drive mad, a harmonica sigh,
And the child feels in time to each slow caress
Rush and recede endlessly the desire to cry.

*Subtitled 'after Rimbaud' in "Breaking and Entering", Oxford 1971.

The Lice Seekers
Arthur Rimbaud (translated by Anthony Weir)

When, full of red torments, the child's troubled head
entreats the white swarm of shadowy dreams,
two gentle grown-up sisters come close to his bed
with fragile fingers like silver-tipped machines.

Before a casement window they sit the child down,
a window open wide to where the azure air
bathes a tangle of flowers, and upon his tousled crown
their terrible, fine fingers move with magical care.

He listens to the sighing of their apprehensive breath
which smells of the long honeys of the flowering earth,
interrupted now and then by a subtle hiss:
saliva caught on the lip, or desire for a kiss.

He hears their black eyelashes flicker overhead
in the sweetsmelling silence, and their sovereign fingers, sweet,
electric in his languidness, meet
in a crackle: little lice are dead.

And there rises in him the wine of listlessness,
delirium-inducing harmonica sigh;
he feels with the slowness of each careful caress
endlessly surging and ebbing the desire to cry.

From The Irish

The Viking Terror
(translated by Brendan Kennelly)

There's a wicked wind tonight,
Wild upheaval in the sea;
No fear now that the Viking hordes
Will terrify me.

'The Bitter Wind is High Tonight'
(translated by Robin Flower)

The bitter wind is high tonight
It lifts the white locks of the sea;
In such wild winter storm no fright
Of savage Viking troubles me.

'Fierce and Wild is the Wind Tonight'
(translated by James Carney)

Fierce and wild is the wind tonight,
it tosses the tresses of the sea to white;
on such a night as this I take my ease;
fierce Northmen only course the quiet seas.

Storm in Uncertain Times
(translated by Anthony Weir)

The winds are bitter tonight; they tear
and wildly toss the sea's white hair.
And yet they bring my mind much ease
for Norsemen sail on calmer seas.

The translations above show the extent of variation between translations, and for comparison other translations from the Irish include: 'Líadain' ('Líadan'), 'The Ex-Poet', 'Ordeal by Cohabitation' ('The Trial of Intimacy'), 'The Sweetness of Nature' ('King Sweeney's Solitude'), 'The Blackbird at Belfast Lough', and 'The Priest Re-discovers his Psalm Book', all by 'Frank O'Connor'; 'The Ivy Crest' ('King Sweeney's "Oratory" '), 'Two Fragments' ('The Blackbird at Belfast Lough'/'The Blackbird'), 'East and By North' ('The Sea in Swell'), all by Robin Flower; 'A Love Song' ('A Kiss'), 'My Story' ('Winter'), both by Brendan Kennelly.

See also 'Gloss, on the Difficulties of Translation', by John Hewitt in *The Planter and the Gael*, published by the Arts Council of Northern Ireland, 1971.

Poems from German, French, Italian, Portuguese and Spanish, including Rilke's *'Archäischer Torso Apollos'* (see Appendix III) and Brecht's 'Concerning a Drowned Girl', Baudelaire's 'Spleen', and *'Harmonie du Soir'* are included in *The Poem Itself*, edited by Stanley Burnshaw, and published in the USA by Holt, Rinehart and Winston in 1960, and in England by Pelican Books, 1964.

See also, for translations from the French, 'Poor People at Church' ('The Poor at Church') translated by Norman Cameron in *Arthur Rimbaud*, published by the Hogarth Press, 1942, and reprinted in *The Penguin Book of Modern Verse Translation*, ed George Steiner, London, 1966, and 'Vowels', translated by F Scott Fitzgerald in *College of One* by Sheila Graham, published by Weidenfeld and Nicholson Ltd and Viking Press Inc. The translation is also included in *The Penguin Book of Modern Verse Translation*. Scott Fitzgerald takes amazing liberties with the poem. A translation of *The Lament of the Fair Hëaulmière* and *The Ballad of Bygone Times*, by Norman Cameron appears in *François Villon - Poems*, published by Johathan Cape, London, 1952. The translation of the first of these two poems also appears in *The Penguin Book of Modern Verse Translation*.

For translation from the Danish see 'The Eternal Three' ('Eternal Triangle'), translated by Martin S Allwood, John Hollander and Inga Allwood, in *The Penguin Book of Modern Verse Translation*, and in *Modern Danish Poems*, ed Knud K Morgensen, Host & Sons, Copenhagen, 1949.

Appendix II: Analysis of a Translation

Au Cabaret Vert
Arthur Rimbaud

A large part of Rimbaud's originality lay in his use of traditional forms to frame violent, shocking or commonplace expressions. He used colloquialisms freely, mixing them with 'poetic' dictions and esoteric words; and although many of his poems are written in strict Alexandrines (his only formal deviation being a deliberate and striking use of enjambment), they read easily, just like natural (if inspired) speech. In translating his sonnets into English it is impossible to retain this contrast between traditional form and easy revolutionary utterance which is part of the point of the poems, and part of Rimbaud's greatness as a poet.

In French (and Danish) it is much easier to find rhymes than in English (or Irish). When translating from Irish one has no compunction about using half-rhymes, for they occur frequently in the originals. But in French the form is often very important and a translator is unhappy with necessary compromises in rhyme and line-length. Even if he were to make a free paraphrase in English the same problem would arise. So translating Rimbaud into English verse is a constant struggle between rhyme, rhythm, line-length and easy flow. Inevitably something of the original is lost, but, in the translations in this book at any rate, I hope that less is lost than in a literal prose translation or in a free paraphrase.

Au Cabaret-Vert appears below in the original French together with a literal prose translation, followed by the various drafts of the translation, whose final form appears earlier in this book.

Au Cabaret-Vert
Cinq heures du soir

Depuis huit jours, j'avais déchiré mes bottines
Aux cailloux des chemins. J'entrais à Charleroi.
-Au Cabaret-Vert: je demandai des tartines
De beurre et du jambon qui fût à moitié froid.

Bienheureux, j'allongeai les jambes sous la table
Verte: je contemplai les sujets très naifs

De la tapisserie. -Et ce fut adorable,
Quand la fille aux tétons énormes, aux yeux vifs,

-Celle-là, ce n'est pas un baiser qui l'épeure!-
Rieuse, m'apporta des tartines de beurre,
Du jambon tiède, dans un plat colorié,

Du jambon rose et blanc parfumé d'une gousse
D'ail, - et m'emplit la chope immense, avec sa mousse
Que dorait un rayon de soleil arrieré.

At the Green Tavern 5 p.m.

For a week I had been tearing my boots to shreds
on the stones of the roads. I walked into Charleroi.
-Into The Green Tavern: I asked for (slices of) bread
and butter and some half-cold ham. Happy, I stretched
out my legs underneath the green table: I studied the naive
patterns on the wallpaper. -And it was marvellous when
the girl with the enormous teats and sparkling eyes (it
isn't a kiss that would frighten that one!) smilingly brought
me bread and butter and lukewarm ham on a coloured
plate - pink and white ham flavoured with a clove of
garlic - and filled me a huge tankard whose froth was made
golden by a shaft of late sunlight.

At The Green Man 5 p.m.

verse 1:   For more than a week I'd been tearing my boots
on the stones of the roads. At 'The Green Man'
in Charleroi I asked for bread and butter, and a plate
of all they had to offer: some half-cold ham.

~~I'd I had been ripping my boots for seven or eight~~
I'd torn my boots to shreds for seven or eight
days on the stones of the roads. At the 'Green Man'
in Charleroi I ordered bread and butter and a plate
of all they had to offer: some half-cold ham.

verse 2:   Happy, I stretched out my ~~legs~~ long legs underneath
the ~~green~~ table. I studied the ~~simple and unfashionable~~ designs
~~unsubtle, undistinguished~~
~~and ingenuous~~
~~and inelegant~~
homely and simple
on the wallpaper - and it was quite a relief
when the girl with huge teats and ~~eager, lively~~ sparkling eyes -
~~when the big bosomed girl with the sparkling eyes -~~
~~breasted~~

Happily I stretched out my legs beneath the green
table. I studied the wallpaper's artless design~~(s).~~
~~And, to complete the whole delightful scene~~
And to make it all perfect ~~an absolute~~ queen
~~an unadorned~~
~~a veritable~~
~~a natural~~
~~a~~
of a girl with ~~huge teats~~ enormous teats and sparkling eyes -

verse 3:   ~~(it would~~ take more than a kiss to ruffle her!)
smilingly brought me my meal of bread and butter
and luke-warm ham set on a coloured platter

(it would take more than a kiss to frighten her!)
- smilingly brought me ~~the~~ my bread and butter there
~~- carried over smilingly the plain and simple fare~~
and the luke-warm ham ~~on~~ set on a coloured plate:
~~ham and bread and butter set on a coloured plate:~~

verse 4: ham pink and white and flavoured with the ~~sheer~~ clear
~~taste~~ tang of garlic - and poured me out a great mug of beer
whose head in the setting sun was golden ~~like~~ as her hair.

ham pink and white and made delicious with a mere
clove of garlic - and filled me a huge mug of beer
with froth turned to gold by a shaft of evening light.

~~ham pink and white and flavoured with a clove~~
~~of garlic - and filled up my tankard whose froth~~
~~was turned to gold by a last shaft of light.~~

ham pink and white and flavoured with the sheer
tang of garlic - and ~~poured me~~ filled up ~~my~~ a ~~great~~ huge mug ~~of~~
with beer
~~tang of garlic - and drew me a huge mugful of beer~~
~~tang of garlic - and brought me a huge mug of beer~~
whose froth was turned to gold by a shaft of evening light.

Appendix III: Paraphrases

The following are poems which I did not feel were translations in the sense that other poems in this book were, although they stick quite close to the originals. They are paraphrases in that the sense of the original has been altered to some extent in one or two lines, though (particularly in the Brecht paraphrase) as a whole the original poem remains, rather like Rilke's Greek Torso, with a chip off here and a smudge on there.

Ancient Torso of Apollo
('Archäischer Torso Apollos' by Rainer Maria Rilke (1875-1926), from *Der Neuen Gedichte anderer Teil*, 1908)

Headless, he still glows, else in the slight
twist of his loins would no smile swerve
and shine from his creative centre; else the curve
his chest makes would not blind you with its light

that gleams as from a wild beast's pelt;
nor, like a candle merely burned down low
would his gaze glint still in his torso;
else this mutilated stump would never melt

the stony hearts of men, radiating far
beyond its broken edges, like a star:
for on this fragment there is no

place that does not look at you
though eyes and head are gone, and strange,
unknowable. Your life must change.

Whore's Song

('Lied eines Freundenmädchens' by Bertolt Brecht (1898-1956), from *The Round Heads and the Pointed Heads*, 1938)

Since I was seventeen
I've been in the love trade
and I've seen plenty,
most of it pretty bad -
but that's the way the cookie crumbles.
Even so, I've been hurt quite a bit -
after all, I'm a human being too.
> *But everything, thank God! is quickly over.*
> *Love and sorrow both disappear.*
> *Where is the sweat that flowed last summer?**
> *Where are the snows of yesteryear?*

Of course it's easy
to break into the love market
when you're only seventeen,
and you swindle a hell of a lot of men.
But feeling keeps on
devaluing inside
when you save it up so hard.
And in any case, every supply runs out sooner or later.
> *But everything, thank God! is quickly over.*
> *Love and sorrow both disappear.*
> *Where is the sweat that flowed last summer?*
> *Where are the snows of yesteryear?*

And so by the time
you've learned all there is
to know in the love business
you won't be able to love
or to make any money -
after all, you aren't seventeen for ever!
> *But everything, thank God! is quickly over.*
> *Love and sorrow both disappear.*
> *Where is the sweat that flowed last summer?*
> *Where are the snows of yesteryear?*

the stony hearts of men, radiating far
beyond its broken edges, like a star:
for on this fragment there is no

place that does not look at you
though eyes and head are gone, and strange,
unknowable. Your life must change.

---

* The most significant departure from the original occurs in the third line of the refrain, which has in the German 'Where are last night's tears?' - a line which could not be included in any form given the necessary rhyme of 'disappear' with 'yesteryear' in the other two lines of the refrain. The last line is essential because it is itself a translation of Villon's *'Ou sont les neiges d'antan?'*, Brecht being a great admirer of Villon.

The Hermit

The following verses are from an eighth or ninth century poem describing the more rigorous aspects of the ascetic life of an Irish hermit.

All alone in my little hut
practising my faith:
dear is it to my heart
my pilgrimage to death.

My cell is hidden and remote;
my eyes are weak with tears
falling for my body's lust;
my conscience strong and clear.

Passions withered up and weak,
rejection of the world,
my thoughts eager, pure and meek -
I seek the grace of God.

Wailing, heartfelt and sincere
up to cloudy Heaven;
fervent showers of tears
and devout confession.

A cold bed gives me no rest
where only the doomed would lie;
my sleep is short and comfortless
before I rise to pray.

My food is merely adequate:
dry bread, and from the hill
clear water — what I eat
is no sinner's fill.

I eat unpalatable food
and study with great care;
I do not visit, do not fight.
My soul is calm and clear.

How holy and how beautiful
to have a leathern skin
and cheeks sunk into the skull,
a body dry and thin!

I would love God's son to come,
my King, to visit me;
my mind to go and dwell with Him
where He dwells perfectly.

Let the place which shelters me
and every holy stone
be a perfect hermitage
and I all alone.

Select Bibliography

Danish

All the published poems I have translated are included in *Dansk Lyrik Fra Gustaf Munch-Petersen til Frank Jæger* published in paperback by Gyldendal, Copenhagen 1962.

French

Two of the Villon poems (those from *The Testament*) are included in *The Penguin Book of French Verse* volume 1, London. 1961, and all three in *The Complete Works of Francois Villon* edited by Anthony Bonner (with full notes) and published by Bantam Dual-Language Books, New York 1964.

Ronsard's '*Quand vous serez bien vieille...*' and the anonymous Rondeau are both in *The Penguin Book of French Verse*, Vols 1 and 2, London 1961. The Baudelaire poems can be found in *Baudelaire: Selected Verse* published by Penguin Books, London 1961, and the Rimbaud poems are included in *Rimbaud: Collected Poems*, also published by Penguin Books, London 1962.

German

The Brecht songs are from the complete edition of Brecht's works published by Suhrkamp Verlag, Frankfurt-am-Main; some are included in a Suhrkamp paperback volume entitled *Gedichte und Lieder aus Stücken*.

Swedish

Lars Huldén's poems come from the collections *Enrönnen*, published by Schildt, Helsinki 1966, and *Herr Varg!* published by Raben and Sjögrén, Stockholm 1969.

Mesopotamian

The texts I have used are from *A Sumerian Reading-book* by C J Gadd, published by the University Press, Oxford 1924. Excellent books on the background to the Mesopotamian poems include: S H Hooks: *Middle Eastern Mythology*. Penguin, London 1963; N.K. Sandars: *The Epic of Gilgamesh*. Penguin, London 1960. *Poems of Heaven and Hell from Ancient Mesopotamia*. Penguin Books, London 1971.

Irish

Comments on and translations of Irish texts may be found in the following:

James Carney: *Studies in Irish Literature and History*. Dublin 1955.
    contributor to *Early Irish Society* ed. Myles Dillon, Dublin 1954 (Paperback)
Robin Flower: *The Irish Tradition*. Oxford 1947.
Kenneth H. Jackson: *A Celtic Miscellany*, Penguin Classics. London 1971.
    Studies in Early Celtic Nature Poetry. Cambridge 1955.
Brendan Kennelly: editor and contributor to *The Penguin Book of Irish Verse*. London 1970.
Kuno Meyer: *King and Hermit*. London 1901.
    Selections from Ancient Irish Poetry. London 1928.
Gerard Murphy (ed): *Early Irish Lyrics*. London 1956.
Eoin Neeson: *Poems from the Irish*. Cork 1967. (Paperback)
Frank O'Connor: *Kings, Lords and Commons*. London.
    The Little Monasteries. Dublin 1963.
    contributor to *The Penguin Book of Modern Verse Translation*. London 1966.
    (with David Greene) *A Golden Treasury of Irish Poetry, AD 600-1200*. London 1967.

Books useful for understanding the background of the Irish translations include:

F.J. Byrne: *Irish Kings and High Kings*. London 1973.
Ludwig Bieler: *Ireland, Harbinger of the Middle Ages*. Oxford 1963. (For the text of 'Cat and Monk' etc.)
James Carney: *Medieval Irish Lyrics*. Dublin 1967.
Myles Dillon: *Early Irish Literature*. Chicago 1948.
Myles Dillon (ed): *Early Irish Society*. Dublin 1954. (Paperback)
Estyn Evans: *The Personality of Ireland*. Cambridge 1973.
Louis Gougaud: *Christianity in Celtic Lands*. London 1932.
Francoise Henry: *Irish Art* (3 vols). London 1965.
Kathleen Hughes: *Early Christian Ireland - An Introduction to the Sources*. London 1972.
Gearoid Mac Niocaill: *Ireland before the Vikings*. Dublin 1972. (Paperback)
Proinsias Mac Cana: *Celtic Mythology*. Paul Hamlyn, London 1970.
Gerard Murphy: *Saga and Myth in Ancient Ireland*. Dublin 1955. (Paperback)
    The Ossianic Lore and Romantic Tales of Medieval Ireland. Dublin 1955. (Paperback)
    (These two books plus Eleanor Knott's *Irish Classical Poetry* are reprinted in *Early Irish Literature* edited by James Carney.)
Donncha O Corrain: *Ireland before the Normans*. Dublin 1972. (Paperback)
Anne Ross: *Pagan Celtic Britain*. Rontledge and Kegan Paul, London 1967 and Cardinal Books, London 1974. Contributor to *Witch Figure* edited by Venetia Newall, Routledge and Kegan Paul, London 1973.

In many of the above mentioned books are excellent and exhaustive Bibliographies.

Index of Titles

Where there is no title to a poem in the text, the first line is given. Poems included in Appendix III are listed in brackets. This index does not include poems by other translators in Appendix I.